Bible Interpretations

Ninth Series
July 2 – September 27, 1893

Acts, Romans

Bible Interpretations

Ninth Series

Acts, Romans

These Bible Interpretations were given during the early eighteen nineties at the Christian Science Theological Seminary at Chicago, Illinois. This Seminary was independent of the First Church of Christ Scientist in Boston, Mass.

By
Emma Curtis Hopkins

President of the Christian Science Theological Seminary at Chicago, Illinois

Bible Interpretations: Ninth Series

By Emma Curtis Hopkins

© WiseWoman Press

Managing Editor: Michael Terranova

ISBN: 978-0945385-59-2

WiseWoman Press

Vancouver, WA 98665

www.wisewomanpress.com

www.emmacurtishopkins.com

CONTENTS

	Editors Note.. vii
	Foreword by Rev. Natalie R. Jean ix
	Introduction by Rev. Michael Terranova................. xi
I.	Secret Of All Power.. 1
	Acts 16: 6-15
II.	The Flame of Spiritual Verity 13
	Acts 16:18
III.	Healing Energy Gifts.. 21
	Acts 18:19-21
IV.	Be Still My Soul... 31
	Acts 17:16-34
V.	Missing 39
	Acts 18:1-11
VI.	Missing 41
	Missing
VII.	The Comforter is the Holy Ghost................... 43
	Acts 20
VIII.	Conscious of a Lofty Purpose 55
	Acts 21
IX.	Measure of Understanding 65
	Acts 26:19-32
X.	The Angels of Paul 81
	Acts 27
XI.	The Hope of Israel 89
	Acts 28:20-31
XII.	Joy in the Holy Ghost 95
	Romans 14
XIII.	REVIEW 103
	Acts 26:19-32
	List of Bible Interpretation Series................117

Editors Note

All lessons starting with the Seventh Series of Bible Interpretations will be Sunday postings from the Inter-Ocean Newspaper in Chicago, Illinois. Many of the lessons in the following series were retrieved from the International New Thought Association Archives, in Mesa, Arizona by, Rev Joanna Rogers. Many others were retrieved from libraries in Chicago, and the Library of Congress, by Rev. Natalie Jean.

All the lessons follow the Sunday School Lesson Plan published in "Peloubet's International Sunday School Lessons". The passages to be studied are selected by an International Committee of traditional Bible Scholars.

Some of the Emma's lessons don't have a title. In these cases the heading will say "Comments and Explanations of the Golden Text," followed by the Bible passages to be studied.

Foreword

By Rev. Natalie R. Jean

I have read many teachings by Emma Curtis Hopkins, but the teachings that touch the very essence of my soul are her Bible Interpretations. There are many books written on the teachings of the Bible, but none can touch the surface of the true messages more than these Bible interpretations. With each word you can feel and see how Spirit spoke through Emma. The mystical interpretations take you on a wonderful journey to Self Realization.

Each passage opens your consciousness to a new awareness of the realities of life. The illusions of life seem to disappear through each interpretation. Emma teaches that we are the key that unlocks the doorway to the light that shines within. She incorporates ideals of other religions into her teachings, in order to understand the commonalities, so that there is a complete understanding of our Oneness. Emma opens our eyes and mind to a better today and exciting future.

Emma Curtis Hopkins, one of the Founders of New Thought teaches us to love ourselves, to speak our Truth, and to focus on our Good. My life has moved in wonderful directions because of her teachings. I know the only thing that can move me in this world is God. May these interpretations guide you to a similar path and may you truly remember that "There Is Good For You and You Ought to Have It."

Introduction

Emma Curtis Hopkins was born in 1849 in Killingsly, Connecticut. She passed on April 8, 1925. Mrs. Hopkins had a marvelous education and could read many of the worlds classical texts in their original language. During her extensive studies she was always able to discover the Universal Truths in each of the world's sacred traditions. She quotes from many of these teachings in her writings. As she was a very private person, we know little about her personal life. What we do know has been gleaned from other people or from the archived writings we have been able to discover.

Emma Curtis Hopkins was one of the greatest influences on the New Thought movement in the United States. She taught over 50,000 people the Universal Truth of knowing "God is All there is." She taught many of founders of early New Thought, and in turn these individuals expanded the influence of her teachings. All of her writings encourage the student to enter into a personal relationship with God. She presses us to deny anything except the Truth of this spiritual Presence in every area of our lives. This is the central focus of all her teachings.

The first six series of Bible Interpretations were presented at her seminary in Chicago, Illinois. The remaining Series', probably close to thirty, were printed in the Inter Ocean Newspaper in Chicago. Many of the lessons are no longer available for various reasons. It is the intention of WiseWoman Press to publish as many of these Bible Interpretations as possible. Our hope is that any missing lessons will be found or directed to us.

I am very honored to join the long line of people that have been involved in publishing Emma Curtis Hopkins's Bible Interpretations. Some confusion exists as to the numbering sequence of the lessons. In the early 1920's many of the lessons were published by the Highwatch Fellowship. Inadvertently the first two lessons were omitted from the numbering system. Rev. Joanna Rogers has corrected this mistake by finding the first two lessons and restoring them to their rightful place in the order. Rev. Rogers has been able to find many of the missing lessons at the International New Thought Alliance archives in Mesa, Arizona. Rev. Rogers painstakingly scoured the archives for the missing lessons as well as for Mrs. Hopkins other works. She has published much of what was discovered. WiseWoman Press is now publishing the correctly numbered series of the Bible Interpretations.

In the early 1940's, there was a resurgence of interest in Emma's works. At that time, Highwatch Fellowship began to publish many of her writings, and it was then that *High Mysticism*, her seminal work was published. Previously, the material contained in High Mysticism was only available as individual lessons and was brought together in book form for the first time. Although there were many errors in these first publications and many Bible verses were incorrectly quoted, I am happy to announce that WiseWoman Press is now publishing *High Mysticism* in the a corrected format. This corrected form was scanned faithfully from the original, individual lessons.

The next person to publish some of the Bible Lessons was Rev. Marge Flotron from the Ministry of Truth International in Chicago, Illinois. She published the Bible Lessons as well as many of Emma's other works. By her initiative, Emma's writings were brought to a larger audience when DeVorss & Company, a longtime publisher of Truth Teachings, took on the publication of her key works.

In addition, Dr. Carmelita Trowbridge, founding minister of The Sanctuary of Truth in Alhambra, California, inspired her assistant minister, Rev. Shirley Lawrence, to publish many of Emma's works, including the first three series of Bible Interpretations. Rev. Lawrence created mail order courses for many of these Series. She has graciously passed on any information she had, in order to assure that these works continue to inspire individuals and groups who are called to further study of the teachings of Mrs. Hopkins.

Finally, a very special acknowledgement goes to Rev Natalie Jean, who has worked diligently to retrieve several of Emma's lessons from the Library of Congress, as well as libraries in Chicago. Rev. Jean hand-typed many of the lessons she found on microfilm. Much of what she found is on her website, www.highwatch.net.

It is with a grateful heart that I am able to pass on these wonderful teachings. I have been studying dear Emma's works for fifteen years. I was introduced to her writings by my mentor and teacher, Rev. Marcia Sutton. I have been overjoyed with the results of delving deeply into these Truth Teachings.

In 2004, I wrote a Sacred Covenant entitled "Resurrecting Emma," and created a website, www.emmacurtishopkins.com. The result of creating this covenant and website has brought many of Emma's works into my hands and has deepened my faith in God. As a result of my love for these works, I was led to become a member of Wise-Woman Press and to publish these wonderful teachings. God is Good.

My understanding of Truth from these divinely inspired teachings keeps bringing great Joy, Freedom, and Peace to my life.

Dear reader; It is with an open heart that I offer these works to you, and I know they will touch you as they have touched me. Together we are living in the Truth that God is truly present, and living for and through each of us.

The greatest Truth Emma presented to us is "My Good is my God, Omnipresent, Omnipotent and Omniscient."

Rev. Michael Terranova
WiseWoman Press
Vancouver, Washington, 2010

LESSON I

Secret Of All Power

Acts 16: 6-15

The Ancient Chinese Doctrine of Taoism

Among the very earliest existing productions of the human mind are the Chinese books of the "Kings." In common with the purely abstract teachings of all ancient sacred books, they agreed in meaning with the Hebrew Bible and Christian testament. In the Christian testament we find the divine being saying, "I can lay down my body and I can take it up again." "I laid down my life that I might take it again; I have the power to lay it down and I have the power to take it again." In the Hebrew Bible the divine being proclaims, "I have spoken and I will bring to pass. I am God and there is none like me."

In the Chinese "Kings" is the doctrine of Taoism, a beautiful accompaniment to the pure metaphysics of Christian Science. The divine being is called Tao, read this:

"The Tao is the unnameable,

and is the origin of heaven and earth.

As that which can be named,

Tao is the mother of all things.

The unnamed and the named are essentially one.

They are being and not-being.

The Tao is inexhaustible purity.

It is not the object of perception.

It is not without desires, great.

All things are born of being.

Being is born of not-being."

On this teaching a student of metaphysics remarks: "By this we see that the philosophy of the Tao-te-King is that of being or not-being, or the ideality of being and not-being. In this point it anticipates Hegel by twenty-three centuries. By it we are taught that the absolute is the source of being and of not-being."

Manifesting of God Powers

As Jesus Christ, the manifest God, could do whatsoever he chose with his life, so can all men, for all came forth from the same God and manifest him to the extent they elect. The Taoism of ancient China brings forward many propositions for manifesting God power and God intelligence. Followed out they are as practicable as the teachings of Jesus, and have the same effect on the mind and life. Read further:

"Being is essence; not-being is the existence.

The first is the nonmenal, the last the phenomenal.

As, being is the source of not being

(the phenomenal or physical),

by identifying one's self with being

one attains to all that is not being, or all that exists.

(He can master it at will).

Instead, therefore, of aiming at acquiring knowledge,

the wise man avoids it: instead of acting, he refuses to act.

He feeds his mind with a wise passiveness.

Not to act is the source of power.

The wise man is like water, which seems weak and is strong,

which yields, seeks the lowest place,

which seems the softest thing and breaks the hardest thing.

To be wise, one must renounce wisdom.

To be good one must renounce justice and humanity.

To be learned one must renounce knowledge.

One must detach himself from all things.

To desire aright is not to desire.

The saint can do great things, because he does not attempt to dothem.

By this negation of all things we come into possession of all things.

Not to act, is therefore the secret of all power.

He who knows the Tao need not fear the bite of serpents nor the laws of wild beasts.

He is inaccessible.

Nothing can hurt him.

He is invulnerable (to age and decay) and he is safe from death."

There are two ways of understanding the doctrine of Jesus Christ. The lesson of today takes up the position of Paul on the question of converting men, and shows the policy of the church militant since Paul's days. Their orders had been direct and peremptory, "Go and teach all nations, baptizing them in the name of the Father and of the Son and of the Holy Ghost." Barnabas had a state of mind continually within him tending to the practicalization of the assurance of Jesus Christ that "My yoke is easy and my burden is light." It is Taoism in respect to action. Paul had the directly opposite state of mind. He felt that the whole universe depended on his activity. Except he exercise himself violently for the gospel, he would not be doing his bounden duty by it. So he and Barnabas separated. Those two types of mind do not work together. The church as it now appears is founded on the Paul type. There is no fulfillment of prophecy except it glory in martyrdom.

Barnabas took John and Mark along with him, and it is related of them that they converted many and healed multitudes by laying the manuscript of

Matthew's on the foreheads of people. They believed so simply in its mastering truths that it did all their work for them. But they established no church and were never heard of afterward. They were too quiet. They lacked the third element essential to two states of mind. A third element emphasizing or expressing their principles being supplied to them and it is certain that their church would have been reigning to-day. Their exemplification of the doctrine of Jesus would have prevailed.

Paul, Timothy, and Silas

Paul and Timothy had their third. They had Silas. His name meant third. If two work together, will they do better if a third suited to them is with them. Silas made a negative of positiveness of Paul and Timothy. These three states of mind may be perfectly balanced in one mind and all the plans may be carried out without comrades.

It is strange that "Taoism," which was what Barnabas was trying to practice, never has yet had a triad in its working representatives. Jesus was the three in one. He never defended himself when attacked, and was docile to the fact that people "hated him without a cause." He taught to turn the left cheek to him that had smitten the right, and to give the cloak to him that had stolen the coat. But Paul knew no such "flabby Christianity". And Barnabas, who tried it literally, not having that other idea which ought to go with it, either as a comrade or a state of mind, made no success of it.

As Silas means lover of the still small voice or listener to the spirit and he made the background for Paul's *alto-relievo* (high relief), we may conclude that those who have practiced like Barnabas and John Mark have never had good listening qualities. They have taken too much of the "say so" of external appearance to heart. Those who cannot listen to spirit well are sensitive to the criticisms of the world. One who hears the still small voice is deaf to the opinions of men. "Who is blind but my servant, or deaf as the messenger I sent: who opened the ears but heard not?"

He who takes this attitude is always successful. He does not have to act in the recognized lines. He is called lucky, but it is only because he listens well. The clergyman's story of Lord Scoresby is a case of pure illustration of how great a fool a man may be from a worldly standpoint, but being intellectually deaf and blind to man's ideas. He is keenly sensitive without explaining it, to the victorious silence whose speech only the Silas or, Scoresby type can hear. They are lucky stars for whatever two associate with them. As a state of mind for you, to hold, whether you believe in exerting yourself like Paul, or having felt that the highest doctrine you have ever heard demands your honorable service, like Timothy, or both united with it, you will always carry out your highest good and never be defeated by anything.

Is Fulfilling as Prophecy

Paul the worker having Silas and Timothy to counterpoise his vengeance tendencies had a clear vision at Troas. This lesson of Acts 16: 6-15, tells the experiences of all hard workers for spiritual propagation. The part that is not told here, viz: about those who are refined and sensitive to criticisms, but believe in spiritual dominion which they have not seen demonstrated (like John Mark) and believe in the comfort and consolation of the gospel of Jesus, though they may have not seen it demonstrated (like Barnabas) is the part that must be lived to be appreciated and whose church is just now for the first time visible pointing its golden spire toward heaven. The third to Barnabas and John Mark, the triad of the Taoists, the new man in the doctrine of "Let Be" is opening his ears to the speech of the absolute and closing them to the ideas of the intellect, whether in Paul's church militant or out of it. Therefore that is unrecorded as history, but is fulfilling as prophecy. Those who realize it are wholly indifferent to the performances of armies. They feel the rush of the angels now marching to establish a kingdom here on earth in full sight of all men, in which there shall be no pain or misfortune.

When Barnabas (the idea that the doctrine of Jesus does not submit its adherents to suffering, but rests them in consolation) and John Mark (the doctrine or idea that there is no pioneering and cruelty where Jesus leads) find their "Silas" (the idea that is not necessary to know anything to know all things) then demonstration is swift. "In such an hour as ye think not the Son of man (the manifestation of good beyond what has been named) cometh."

In this history of the believer of work who is honorable in his calling and lets the inner prompting always have sway when it is felt, we have his way, and your history section by section and the history of the church, period by period. You feel to go one way; it is hedged in. You essay to go another; it is impossible. You fret, but you conclude the spirit hindered for a better move. Then the way is plain. Before you; so plain you cannot mistake it. You go in it obediently. You accomplish a mission. You find your peace for a time. Then you set forth on another undertaking. Its history is the same.

The church has had the same oasis in her desert marshes. All because she took Paul's triad and did not investigate Jesus Christ's triad, which Barnabas felt, but could not demonstrate, because he left out the third principle of power, viz: "Silas," who hears and believes neither in love or hate, justice or injustice, action or inaction, peace or discord; he is so entranced by the voice. Neither he who believes in the doctrine of Christ as the consolation and peace, nor he who believes in it as tribulation and warfare accomplishes anything without a good faculty for knowing what is prompting him and what -way it pushes. If one is in the heat of the conflict he has brought on himself by insisting on violent efforts to establish peace on earth he will go "through Phrygia and the region of Galatia" — through a long or short experience of barren effort and while, unsupplied thinking, during which experience he prays much and wondered at the seeming unprofitableness of his best efforts. His ways and means do not count favorably.

The Inner Prompting

You who have believed in trying very hard to convert people have all this experience. If you were trying to establish a church or school it was the same. The Silas quality of your mind, or the Silas comrade of your understanding, has not yet got into his place as background for your purposes to stand out in demonstration. You will not get into any difficulties out of which you cannot come easily. Paul and his two companions could not preach the word in Asia, the place of bogs and mud. You who believe in eager efforts, so unlike the peaceable Jesus and the sweet-spirited Taoists are sure to come into conditions of experience which will make you seem abominable to your neighbors, may be even criminal, because you are acting out what the inner prompting compels. This prompting has for its principle of action: "If you take a line of procedure that line has its best methods. I will prompt you on best methods. I will tell Joshua how to raze the walls of Jericho. I will tell the Taoists how to let the walls be and oppose them not. If you will choose your line, I will assist. If you will not choose your line, I will choose for you, and thus you shall be most like Jesus."

Carlyle said; "The situation that hath not its duty, its ideal, was never yet occupied by man." It is the duty, the ideal performance in a situation that the inner prompting gives. The situation into which you have plunged yourself by your belief out of which you are working by the impelling of spirit is called "mysia" in Paul's journey. The strugglers to do right have one great tendency common to them all. If you have always been trying to do right, you have the same impulse. It is the natural voice when condemned for doing your very divinest prompting urged, to act precipitately, to explain yourself hastily to do something violent. In Paul's journey this is called his assaying to "go into Bithynia." The word means violent precipitation, and he assayed to go there. There was a general feeling that he had made a mistake. The spirit never makes mistakes. If you are in any situation, the spirit will take you through it wisely. Give your own spiritual inner judgment the credit of never making mistakes and of always bringing you out safely.

The three who worked well together "came down to Troas." Their time for plain sight and hearing of the right way to be had come, Paul's visions both appeared plainly and spoke clearly. It was the call of his whole realm of discouraged and prostrated thoughts to his will to give the most elevating and inspiring affirmations. "Come over to Macedonia and help us." The Hebrew for that word is "prostrated." The Greek is "elevated, eminent." Sometimes being steadily frustrated depresses a great worker.

Good Taoist Never Depressed

A good Taoist is never depressed. At such times the cool high language of the science uplifts as in eagles' pinions. The studies of scripture being both physical and metaphysical we must take the metaphysical descriptions as well as the dry historic accounts. Then, again, he stopped seeing and hearing the spirit in bodily presence. He came again into loneliness. The path of a worker has many sandy islands. Luther was made so sorrowful by his periods of unrecognized toil that his - wife dressed one day in mourning, as she explained thinking God might be dead. Luther needed more of the Silas indifference to evil and good.

Laying down regard for both evil and good is laying down the life. It is the rest of the soul to lay down regard for either good or evil. Then a great strength came to Paul. He abode in that strength certain days. During that period of strength which followed his working without results for so long he prayed and rested in his prayers. Then the whole fruitage of his thoughts and struggles came in full purple splendor. Give your moments of strength to laying out in beautiful language before the ever present spirit, the description of what you would like to see brought to pass. Solomon's answered prayer came because he spread out his case before the Almighty while he was strong and buoyant.

Jesus Christ said that when he came as the strength and joy of the spirit to his disciples they should ask what they would and it should be done unto them. Every inch of ground gained by the religion of the dominating churches since Paul's time was won by exactly these few movements on the part of the warriors of Christianity. They have earned their laurels by savage courses. Meanwhile Barnabas was healing the multitudes and comforting hearts, but making no noise and seemingly gaining no ground. Out of Paul's policy has grown a powerful and splendid church which has no healing elixirs and has not the remotest idea of how Jesus Christ's gospel to the poor should be expressed so as to relieve the burdened fathers and feed the wan millions now, this instant which he meant his church to do.

Lift up your heads, ye gates of hope, for now is that way coming toward us like an army with banners. Barnabas has found Silas. The unchronicled minister is the true church.

Inter Ocean Newspaper, July 2, 1893

LESSON II

The Flame of Spiritual Verity

Acts 16:18

On the principle of capillary attraction, oil creeps up the strands of a lampwick to feed the illuminating flame. As all things are symbols of mind, life, spirit, so is the operation of the oil with a lampwick and flame. The mind of man is the strand which he dips downward toward some reservoir for what shall keep the flame he calls life burning.

He may dip the strands of his mind into whatsoever reservoir he pleases to furnish his life flame with. He may dip into delusions and keep up a fictitious life. Then he will be dissatisfied with his life flame. He will almost hate what he calls his life.

There is only one reservoir for the strands to dip into that will supply a perfectly satisfactory life flame. There is no limit to its supply. There is no end to the life flame it sets burning. There is no telling the beauty and majesty of the life it causes to light the earth with. That reservoir is spiritual verity.

The lesson to-day mentions some men who had dipped the strands of their mind into the delusion that they must live by the gains they got from the wild speeches of an obsessed girl, and the two who had dipped the strands of their mind into the delusion that they fixed by putting down such false methods of supplying life flames.

Cause of Contention

Then the fight began. There is always a fight going on where there are two delusive pools in juxtaposition. There is never any fight between those who feed their life flame from the oil spring that makes life joyous. The men who felt themselves wronged by Paul and Silas "caught them and drew them into the market place unto the rulers." They resented the loss of their money. This was the natural next step of experience for those minds that had so strongly believed that the "Macedonians" needed their help. It is a sure precursor of trouble on account of financial or ambitious considerations when any mind dips its strands into the delusion that people need help of any kind. The spiritual verity is that nobody needs help. Nobody needs anything. All were supplied in the beginning with all things. If any mind dips into this placid fountain it will cause a sweet life flame to burn whose warmth and beauty will do more converting than all the Paul types in creation.

Nevertheless, Paul's mind strands were leaning toward the spiritual manner of living, and so he came unhurt through the clutches of his opponents. The men, "seeing that hope of their gains was gone, caught Paul and Silas." They called them the worst names they could think of. They called them "Jews." That was a very bad reputation to have in those days.

Delusive Doctrines

Somewhat later than Paul's time Christians were haled to prisons on charge of burning children and holding thyestian banquets. We see by these fierce experiences that leaning toward the spiritual reservoir with the mind does not yield a joyous life, 'tis only by dipping straight down into foundation truths that unassailable, satisfactory life is demonstrated. It is a delusion which leans toward goodness side to imagine that we have a great work to do, a special call of some kind, but it gets us into straits. It gives us the opposition of all that we oppose. God has finished his work. There is nothing that seems undone, but what seems as by reason of the delusive doctrine that there is mighty much good needed to be done.

Into the city which lieth four square here in our midst there never entereth one that "maketh a lie." They bring the glory and honor of the nations into it when they step their feet in. The truth is that all is right now. It does not need to be set right. This is the way that God looks at all that is. Looking at all the nations with this mind is glorifying them and honoring them. It makes the life a delight. The kingdom of heaven is in our midst. Have you tried taking this view of the universe? They made Paul's feet fast in the stocks of his prison. There are prisoners of poverty, prisoners of sickness, prisoners of deformity, prisoners of grief, with their understanding of why God permits them to be afflicted so long and so hard, held fast in the stocks of wonder and amazement.

Paul's History

They say they cannot understand it, for they have lived as carefully and righteously as they knew how going down into their Macedonia of trying to help everybody they met. Paul's history is the one for them to see themselves pictured in. What seemed to be his virtue was his cause for imprisonment, hunger, pain, darkness. He looked upon his world as all wrong. He had a great call to set things right. He must live by that principle exactly as the sorcerers lived by the obsessed girl. His life flame was as fictitious as theirs.

He left Timothy behind. Why? Because this is an object lesson for us. When we are in the heat of the battle brought on by our delusions we forget to consider whether it is honorable for us to get through and out of the battle or not. We only think of getting through and out or enduring as best we can. Timothy signifies "for honor's sake."

Paul kept Silas with him. He who has let his mind dip from the fountain of supposition that he has a great work to do to help the Almighty in perfecting his miserable world always carries a good amount of simple trust in being guided and upheld in his undertaking. Silas means "simple trust."

Silas and Paul together in your mind will make you sing in the midst of tribulations. A great resolve united with a simple trust will quicken song. If this song rises so loud and clear while you are going through your sorrows that other prisoners listen and love your words, as those did in the dungeons near Paul, you will strike the keynote of the prison-house into which you are walled, whether of sickness, poverty, or grief, and the doors will spring open. Your will be free.

Keynotes

A body resounds when its keynote is struck. Sustain the note and it must be jarred to pieces. Joshua sustained the keynote of the walls of Jericho till they tumbled down.

The keynote of poverty can be struck hard against, either by some sweep of ecstatic prayer over the harp strings of the soul's high faith, or by singing high notes with words of Jehovah's sincere praise.

The keynote of sickness may be struck hard against by the prayer of faith that soars so far above the memory of sickness that its fall breaks the walls of the prison-house of sickness.

There's a note which, sustained, would shatter your grief, spreading it to the winds of oblivion. It can be found among the high tones of the songs that praise Jehovah the truest.

There's a lofty note to fall back on the dungeon roof of your hard affairs. You can find it somewhere in the psalms praising the ways of God with his people or on the winged affirmations of Christian Science. You repeat them looking upward as Paul and Silas looked upward, till their meanings are all that your mind can remember.

You are most persistent 'when your night is darkest. Only those who are trying to keep their life flame burning by drawing from the delusions of sense, formulated by dreams of what might be if God were.

Doctrine Not New

This is no new doctrine. When the mind first imagined what might be if good were not all, it is still held to its memory that there is only one being in heaven and on earth and under the earth. The oldest religious philosophy of the world wrote in the rocks that time might not erase the remembrance of truth, that the world that changes and fades is not being. It is appearance without reality, a delusive show. Existence has an essence, a substance, eternal spirit. That is being; reality. It is a well of water springing up into everlasting life. It is the oil of healing. It is the anointing oil of the kings and priests of Christ Jesus, who lived by the knowledge of his mind's ability in common with every other man's ability to draw mighty thoughts and absolute peace from the spirit with which to be a healing presence without knowing or believing that there is healing to be done; an uplifting presence without admitting that there may be any depressed burden-bearers; a holy presence while not finding sin among men; a forerunner of the New Jerusalem through sight of goodness and greatness and spiritual wisdom in all men and all things, everywhere, thinking of evil in none. He who gets into a prison of pain or poverty or sickness through drawing from the reservoirs of delusion may get free by dropping his delusions and dipping into the perfect doctrine that all is well. He who knows the perfect doctrine will never be walled into a prison-house of even regret or fear or dread. He is free born. His feet are shod with freedom. His life is the light of the world.

Inter Ocean Newspaper, July 9, 1983

LESSON III

Healing Energy Gifts

Acts 18:19-21

In the Nouvelle Revue of May 15, M. Delacroix describes the religious attitude of the seventeenth century toward Satan and the gift of healing. "At that time," he says, "the real aristocracy, the most tyrannical, the most feared, and the most influential was Satan. He accomplished prodigies, was master of elements, and disposed of the health, of the fortune, and of the life of men."

The one whom the clergy felt to be most in league with his imaginary being was the Irish prophet Greatriks, or Greatrakes, who was the son of a most respectable Irish family, but about the year 1662 had a revelation of the manner in which the sick are cured by touch. He proclaimed that God had revealed to him that all sickness was a form of obsession, and in order to get well all sick people must get rid of their devil. People flocked to him from all parts; both town and country magistrates invited him to come and heal their sick. The king sent for him at Whitehall and the whole court were astounded at his miracles. The crowd at the French embassy, M. de Comings, ambassador, was so great that it was with difficulty visitors watching his prodigious deeds of healing could pass in and out according to rank.

The chief formula used by Greatricks ran thus: "Foolish spirit, who hast quitted your abode in the waters to come and afflict this body, I order you to issue forth and to return whence you came." Thousands were relieved of their burden of deformity, pain and disease at the sound of this command.

How Paul Healed

While Paul was at Ephesus his aprons and handkerchiefs being touched by the sick caused their maladies to depart. But many in Ephesus, instead of being pleased and won over to believing in the gospel preached by him, believed that instead he was possessed of evil and being "hardened against him spoke of evil of his way before the multitude." Paul in his turn preached so powerfully of every way of healing, except his own, being of the devil, that his converts burned $50,000 worth of formulas and charmed bits of silver, though with them they had wrought the astonishing miracles. He did not while considering their remarkable cures and other miracles to be certainly of the evil one, remember that every good gift is from above. Jesus had not answered the people who thought he cured by the inspiration of Beelzebub by insisting that they were certainly cured by that energy, but his own cures were of divine goodness. He gave his audience to understand that their children could not work miracles except by the power of God.

After Corinth always comes Ephesus — that is, after being driven into close pressure by sordid conditions of seeming failure and coming out victorious through spiritual light and substantial aid, such as Paul received at Corinth, the power of the Holy Ghost in miracle-working begins to be visible in strong measure. Nobody ever wrought miracles under a heavy state of disappointment.

Shall I continue to preach a gospel which does not seem to take care of me by its own inherent kindness? Can I preach of protection, who am not protected? Can I boldly proclaim that it is bread and meat and wine when I am driven to my old trade of tent making and cannot even be listened to if I speak? What must I answer to these questions? Paul at Corinth taught us. I must let the spirit take care of me in its own way. This is trust. If I am too wildly exalted to let go of my efforts I must send for a Silas, which means that one who has simple trust must stay near me till my inward possibility for trusting is warmed forth out of its gloomy soil in my mind. I must call for Timothy, who represents steadfast honor, or I must rouse myself to speak more boldly than ever when I am most poorly provided for. Then I shall, like Paul, hear the living voice of the angel of God's presence. This is substantial help; whether it come by dream or vision new provision is at hand when the angel talks with me. We are all in Corinth sooner or later on our pilgrimage. The support question and the protection question must be settled. Then comes the Ephesus.

To Work Miracles

At Ephesus we must work miracles. We can work miracles for we are in the land of miracle working. Then comes a period when we associate with people who cure great numbers of sick and hungry folks by little amulets and charms like powders and pills and charitable institutions. Shall we be so filled and thrilled with our own high thoughts that we cannot have the heart to condemn their little bottles of medicine and physicians' formulae, their charities, schools and workhouse policies? Are we so entirely absorbed in our doctrine that we cannot see anything but the good working through all these things feeling that there is but one power only which brings comfort and help, whether it be through a pill box or the handkerchief of a Paul.

When Paul was confronted by John's disciples, who had never been told that all power is one, and if recognized as one it increases to such force that the most astonishing miracles may be wrought, he did not speak contemptuously of John's teaching. He spoke with unaffected gentleness. "John said that Jesus Christ should come in the future, but Jesus himself teaches that Christ is already come in all men now with power." This attitude of mind lifted him out of the thought of the government of Satan. He forgot for a while that he believed in Satan. And this was the spreading of his spirit abroad over the multitudes so that they passed his clothing piece by piece over the heads of the crowds, and the lame, and blind and sick touched them and were healed.

While he was in this exalted state of mind he wrote the sixteenth chapter of I. Corinthians. Over the heads of the multitude of years between his transfiguring exaltation of mind and today those chapters are passed down to us who need healing of poverty, pain, deformity, and we may touch them with our attention of mind and be healed.

Paul had his greatest inspiration of power while he was in the school of Tyrannus at Ephesus. It was the princely signal of sonship from Jehovah he was given; therefore he was domiciled with one whose name means prince, or one who reigns. This quality of dignity must be nourished in Paul, for with all this marvelous exhibition of power from the holy spirit he was afraid he would be a castaway from its power.

Paul Worked in Fear

He believed to the last in loss and gain. He believed that he must work desperately to gain the spirit and work desperately lest he lose it. Now, one of the most comforting messages of the Holy Spirit in whomsoever it is acknowledged is its unfailing promise. "The Lord shall fight for you and ye shall hold your peace." There is nothing to be done to help or hinder the power of God. We do our duty by thinking what is true at its highest and lift our hands to the toil nearest at hand, but none of it helps or hinders the Spirit. It bloweth where it listeth. There is one result from knowing this. It never fails to come to pass that we become entirely absorbed in the teaching that the charm of the amulet is the good spirit of God as the charm of a spiritual thought is the Holy Ghost. Then we do not watch the pill box or the bottle for our healing, nor the handkerchief of a great healer. We watch in Spirit only. Then the genius for miracle working breaks forth. All whom we touch "Speak -with tongues and prophecy," whether we touch them with our hands or our thoughts.

Hands are signals. Thoughts are signals. All things are signals that the spirit is nigh, even at our gates. The power of the Holy Ghost is sure to come upon all who have risen up in high resolve to speak what is the highest doctrine they have ever heard or thought of, and put down their struggling for a state of meek trust to take possession of their mind. We shall all come into Ephesus. We shall abide with the reigning powers. We shall, for as long season as we are absorbed in watching the spirit power, have healing energy. Paul got to fearing he might be a castaway. We need fear no loss of that spirit that keeps near us through the eternities. Nothing is lost which is ours. Between Paul and the spirit he was afraid he should lose, there was only his fear that he should lose it.

Shakespeare's Idea of Loss

Shakespeare's idea of the loss of power and greatness, of friendships and possessions is not spoken as the spirit speaks:

"This is the state of man: to-day he puts forth

The tender leaves of hope: to-morrow blossoms

And bears his blushing honors thick upon him.

The third day comes a frost, a killing frost,

And when he thinks, good, easy man, full surely

His greatness is a-ripening, nips his root

And then he falls."

Shakespeare speaks forever from the standpoint of observation of the results of thoughts, and not from the standpoint of what is true regardless of thoughts. "I will never leave thee nor forsake thee" is the truth. "Call and I will answer."

Do you think your strength is lost? It is right near us forever. Take away your idea that your strength is gone and you will see that it is there. Do you think your intelligence is gone? Take away your idea and you will see that as Paul could not be a castaway so you cannot lose the everywhere knowledge of your spirit. Do you think youth and light and possessions are gone? Take away that idea from between you and your happy substance.

Did the imagination of a whole world full of people finally win the race you made of trying to keep your precious goods so that the long belief of the ages in loss and absence became your belief? That was the right thought of man. The morning is broken when race thoughts cannot win with us for the truth is recognized. You need not get off the track of your early thoughts that vigor and beauty would last forever. Koch was beaten off his track of thinking he could cure by the good powers working through lymph. So he failed. Whoever lets his mind get beaten off the track of its first thought that strength and life and opportunity will last forever, will seem to lose them. But why should he let a race belief beat him? We sometimes hear people telling of having lost their love of the spiritual life or their love of their early friends. "That was not love which went." Love is here in changeless steadfastness. Drop the idea that it is lost and its old glory is felt in new life.

Keep on at Ephesus. It is the place from whence power radiates. Paul stayed two years. It is there while forgetting about being a castaway and rising away from the memory of Satan, that Paul's mighty genius rose in splendor. He was past fifty years old when it burned like a light of beauty. The secret of its freedom through him was his forgetfulness of evil and his absorption in his mighty theme. He let Silas go back to Jerusalem for he kept faith enough alive in himself not to need Silas. He kept Timothy for his high resolves were always falling down into depressions and Timothy's steadfastness of honor strengthened them.

Endurance the Sign of Power

The finest mind is the enduring mind. It is the sign of the presence of great power with the idea of failure or loss taken away when there is long holding out. The horse that has no Arabian ancestry may have speed for a mile, but the horses that spring from Arabia have speed all the way.

David's genius came straight from Jehovah. Thus it endured till he caught the race idea of death. There is a picture of David playing before Saul. The harp strings do not hinder or help his music. He knows not Saul's favor or disfavor. The sounds that strike on his inner ears are the strains of choirs that sing to their lovers. His love never failed. Had his ears caught the songs of life that are now being sung he could not have hidden his life behind the veil of his idea that life could fail. Paul held before himself the idea of the loss if his spirit of power and held it so faithfully that he wove a thick veil, but he worked so faithfully to rend the veil that he shouted "There is laid up for me a crown of life." Why not lay aside the rags of long ages of belief in loss and failure of what cannot be lost? Why not lay aside the idea that some good works are of Satan? Why not see that there is but one that works good? Why hate the charms and the formulas more than the words? Are they not all signals of the presence that is changeless good?

The priests in Greatrake's time thought themselves right and him wrong. Paul thought the sorcerers wrong and himself right. Moses thought if he threw up ashes and pronounced boils with blains in the dust thereof for the Egyptians that he was right, but if any of the rest of the Jews undertook to pronounce through symbols they were using enchantments of necromancy and were abominable in the sight of the Almighty. He who marks distinctions is putting up walls and fences. He makes poor and rich feel hatred of each other. He makes wise and foolish think there is difference of spirit within them. It is truth to say that the life of the snake and the life of Moses is one life; the intelligence of the snail and of Abraham is one intelligence, for the one intelligence of the universe bestows not more of himself in one signal than another. Paul at Ephesus teaches this lesson.

Inter Ocean Newspaper July 16, 1893

LESSON IV

Be Still My Soul

Acts 17:16-34

Nothing can be so active as that which is in every place at the same instant. Nobody can be so instantaneous as he who is doing all things this instant. That which is in all places at the same second, and he is doing everything the same moment, must be the stillest of all that moves and works, so there is no inconsistency in speaking of the swift action of soul and the supreme stillness of soul. "Be swift, my soul to conquer," and "Be still my soul," mean the same. The fine fleet light which the ancient mystic got glimpses of as pervading all things, seemed often the limpid principle of absolute inaction. When either way, the fleet of the still, is very appreciable to use we do not need to trust even God, neither do we need to choose our course of action. The sight of the swift Being who is in all places, doing all things at the same instant, relieves us of demonstration in every particular. "In thy light shall we see light."

He would symbolize that he is under no obligation either to abide in trust or to work out his salvation, will leave Silas and Timothy behind and fall in with every wind of circumstance. As it is told of Paul that he did when called to preach in Athens and Corinth. The very description of the power of the universe given here in this chapter as Paul's inspired address before the epicureans and stoics of Greece, A.D. 52, shows that he had seen with his inner vision the instantaneous principle as the everywhere present impulse of all things. "To the unknown God" I call your attention. "Him declare I unto you. He made the world and all things therein of one blood all the nations." Now, "feel after him, for he is not far from everyone of us."

Seeing Is Believing

Paul had seen, and seeing was believing. And seeing was power, so he was sufficient unto himself, he had no need of companions. The more spiritually minded anybody is the less he needs companionship, the less friends and enemies and surroundings move him. He has the fine rest of Silas and the noble honor of Timothy in his own quality; what does he need of their bodily representatives?

It was the Athenians with their 80,000 gods that Paul, who had caught sight of the one God, was called to preach. The Greeks thought strength was embodied in a different god from what health was embodied in. They thought love was incased within a different god from what life was incased within, so they imagined with more concentrated ideals of beauty and strength than any other people ever did. The world has never seen such pictures of beauty and life as the marbles of Phidias, who was known as the "sculptor of the gods," and of the buried authors of the entrancing studies in the Vatican, the gardens of the Medici, and the Florentine galleries. Focusing their mental vision to beauty the devout Greeks formulated beauty. Focusing to life they made the marbles live. But they still felt that far away from their noblest ideals lived a god to whom they owed allegiance, and so in many spots were altars erected with the inscription written upon them, "To the Unknown God." We have now as many gods as we have people from whom it is hard to be parted, or ambitions whose failures are disappointments, and nobody can preach unto us the one God with any bread to our everlasting craving for satisfaction who has to lug around his father, his mother, his wife, or children, or friends, or his ambitions, in other words, his Silases and Timothys, like Paul (at first); or his statues, like the Athenians, or be lonely and unnatural without them. People with ambitions worship gods invisible, like the Greeks. People with attachments to people worship visible gods. Neither of these classes has seen the fleet light that is everywhere this instant, forming and moving everything. Therefore our deepest need for quick ministry of one who is utterly weaned from gods had no preacher.

Paul Stood Alone

If one stands before us preaching that it is truth's ministry to fail not, in kindness and meekness forever, while his heart is quick to turn from fealty it is not in his light that we see light, but in our sight of the light he tells of. If one tells of giving up attachments to kindred as divine science who cannot abide away from his kindred without misery we must see the freedom of spirit itself from dependence, we cannot see independence through the speaker's light on the subject.

Paul stood alone and free, letting the streaming glory of the unhindered spirit be and the maker of words at the same instant. With this attitude of mind only could he master the civilization of polytheism. And this is the only attitude of mind that can master the polytheism of our age. It is not the reality of any life that if it cannot be gratified in one line it is miserable. It was not the reality of life that the marbles embodied. These things are gods. There is one unformulated god who is reality here and in all places now.

Looking away from the god who held all the beauty of heaven within his being while he excluded the goodness of heaven to beauty itself, as there and here and in all places at once, the Greeks, through detachment from forms felt the presence of goodness.

The "unknown God" unto whom their altars were erected was pure, impartial goodness, not more life than strength, and not more beauty than kindness. All these in one. They had but vaguely felt what goodness was so they vaguely named it "unknown."

There is within man the visionary power of looking away from forms to the formless. When he looks back again he sees a new world. To Paul for a short space of looking away the ability to talk to the Stoic and Epicurean philosophers was given as an easy task. To all who detach mind from the formed to the unformed absolute there is sure ability to do without obligation to do, and confidence so simple and sincere that they do not think of their trust, and with these sweeps of the infinite through their faculties great tasks are easy and masterful deeds are light. This Paul demonstrated.

Lessons for the Athenians

He gave his third lesson in Christian science to the Athenians from the platform on the summit of Mars' hill where were assembled "the noblest blood of Athens, the first politicians, the first orators, the first philosophers; a court the most august, not only of Athens but of Greece and indeed of the whole world." It was at this bar Socrates had been arraigned and condemned on the ground of innovating upon the State religion.

Paul had caught the illumination of free universal spirit, and his address aroused his audience to look away from him to his doctrine in which many believed from that moment, but some mocked, and others said, "We will hear thee again of this matter," which is exactly the way the third lessons of the doctrine of Jesus is always received. It teaches the resurrection and the ascension which seems entirely impossible while we look at the world from the standpoint of calling reality what appears to be and believing in what claims to be, while yet it is nothing. Socrates still saw the gods as real after his strained vision toward the real, though all things were changed to him because of his effort. Paul saw no reality on them for he had seen the Real. His vision of the formless had lasted him long enough so that he could not be touched by the laws of Athens. "He who undistracted contemplates me, is me."

All Under His Power

Curses and condemnations fly past those who contemplate upon the speed of that which is in all places this instant. They cannot wound with the tongues or with arrows the character or body of one who sees there is only One who is doing all things this moment. For him there is safe conduct over the earth from sea to sea and from city to city. By undistracted gaze upon that which is meant by the third lesson of Christ Jesus, the whole aspect of nature and humanity changes.

"I will overturn, overturn, overturn, until he whose right it is to reign shall come, and I will give it to him." It is the right of him who looks away from his gods to the one God whose power has no cruelty, no sternness in it to reign. The word shall appear according to his dictum, while the world that now moves panic and disappointment, poverty and blindness past our gaze must pass away as a dream that is told. "I will make the rivers islands and I will dry up the pools. And I will bring the blind by a way that they know not: I will lead them in paths that they have not known; I will make darkness light before them and crooked things straight."

Who will transform the world to our vision? The name of the "unknown God" declared, and the splendor of such goodness as never hurts or permits death or faintness proclaimed, till the sight of his presence is clear on our gaze. If the conflicts of trade and the changes of destiny have woven their nets of trial around you there is sure extrication and peace for you in saying often what you cannot help feeling is true, viz: "Nothing is so swift as that which is in all places at once. God here at my hand is in all places now.

Freedom of Spirit

"Nothing is so free as my free spirit, which is God doing all things now." "The blessing of the Lord it maketh rich and he addeth no sorrow with it." This is the "unknown God" whom Paul saw making the universe and abiding in all places as the same instant. Such sight caused the gods of Greece to become myths. Such sight will set this age free from its multitude of gods. Do you not feel the yellow god gold fast losing his hold on the hearts of men? Do you not see the grip of the ambitions of mankind relaxing? Do you not see what is now taking place subtly as the dew falls and irresistibly as the sun rises? Nothing righteous or faithful can you do among the gods you now worship, whether it is your friendships or your hopes and tastes that you serve will have any reward in it for you. There is no buy or sell, reward or revenge among them all. Steady, undistracted recognition of that which is now in all places doing all things this instant has for its treatment in response to your gaze, first the absolute peace of your own life, and next the extrication of all the race from what seems to be hardship and anguish.

The extrication of man from affliction is only setting him free from his idolatries. His idols are the things he feels himself to be miserable without. Detached from these forms he ascends. Uncumbered by ambitions and wishes he is resurrected. This is the way of the judgment for him. It is the judgment of truth and good that now is come the kingdom here and there upon earth as in heaven.

Inter Ocean Newspaper July 23, 1893

Lesson V

Missing

Paul at Corinth

Acts 18:1-11

Lesson VI

Missing

Paul at Miletus

Acts 20: 22-35

LESSON VII

The Comforter is the Holy Ghost

Acts 20

There is a little book called. "The A.B.C. of the Way." In it is this paragraph: "Whenever man thinks of the blessings and joys that surround him his soul becomes joyous and buoyant. Then a positive spirit takes possession of him, and if he is sick he is healed, and whatsoever he is undertaking prospers. It is certain that good luck comes in at laughing gate. But contrariwise, when one is always complaining — "this is very disagreeable, that is very sad," etc., then the mind becomes negative and death probably results; also whatsoever he has undertaken is unfortunate — is attended with difficulty and failure.

Our lesson today, as is true of all Scripture lessons, makes a man of one overpowering trait of character illustrate how that name trait always works itself out in him that possesses it. Paul, as we have seen by the last three lessons, believed one thing to the extent of its being dominant over every other belief, viz., that the only way to serve the kingdom of heaven was to exert himself to death.

This belief caused him to take his affairs out of the jurisdiction of the Holy Ghost time and again and necessitated his putting language and purposes into the mouth of the Holy Ghost diametrically opposite to what, according to Jesus Christ, it was capable of speaking or purposing.

Jesus had said with great distinctness "The Comforter is the Holy Ghost," and when Paul was in abject misery because of seeming failure along every line he had undertaken, the Holy Ghost had formulated for his sake and had spoken audibly to him this comforting promise: "Be not afraid I am with thee, and no man shall set on thee to hurt thee."

But Paul's own private belief was so indestructible that in spite that divine assurance he told the ministers of Ephesus, who hung on his teaching as law and gospel, that "the Holy Ghost witnesseth in every city, saying that bonds and afflictions await us."

Requisite for an Orator

A heathen philosopher declared that the first requisite for an orator is that he should be a good man. The Christian philosopher must put it that the first requisite for an orator is that he should be a consistent man, one link of his principles must weld, to the next link reasonably.

Was ever the Holy Ghost found telling anything to any man except kindness, peace, protection, beauty? What good is prayer if its answer is "Thou shalt be murdered?" What reliability can be expected from a Holy Ghost which promises no man shall hurt thee," and "bonds and. afflictions await thee?"

What dependence can I place upon the intelligence and fidelity of the Omnipotent if, formulating for my sake after practicing Paul's formulas, it suddenly lights me with hope and as suddenly, *ignis fatuus* (something that misleads) like, darkens me with what the devout Peloubot calls the prophecy of "some dark unknown, calamity?"

Is not such an inconsistent Ghost a dangerous acquaintance? Do you not naturally shrink from one who is to-day your friend, tomorrow your traducer, the next day your friend again?

There is nothing more certain than that Paul's ruling idea of life pioneered him everywhere and was only chloroformed into silence once in a while, not transmuted ever into the positive Spirit which brings safety and success at every turn.

We cannot ignore the fact that the moment Paul gave away his idea of death as the natural result of listening to the Holy Ghost gospel he brought Tichylus back to life, who fell out of a window in a sleep brought on by Paul's long preaching, and "was taken up for dead."

We do not forget how Madame Guyon healed "the sick unto death;" as they were called, when her belief which exactly corresponded with Paul's on the matter of tortures, bonds, death, suddenly faltered before her faith in the life and health dealing nature of Spirit.

What is a Myth

Who set that idea going that opposition to Spirit finally conquers in this world? Did not the strong believer in the opposite of good know that any belief like that is a cyclone going through the mind stratum that lies close to the ears of mankind and when it whistles and blows its propositions close at the hearing faculty it makes men think they hear people telling of woes and troubles? If you fear that the Lord intends trouble for you, do you know where you got that fear? You got it from Paul, who got it from the prophets, who got it from Adam; they never got it from God. And who was Adam? A myth. What is a myth? It is the story of something that never took place.

Did not Adam exist? No. What was he? He was the shadow of a substance. A shadow is nothing. "All flesh is the shadow that declineth."

Are not the roses real? Not the roses that wither and die. In that day was made, "every plant of the field which was made before it was in the earth." That plant which was made before it was in the earth is the real rose. It has no worms or moths to destroy its life or its beauty. The same with man. His soul is his indestructible life in its immortal beauty. It was to that; Paul listened, and it told of fearless life. It was to the myth about his soul that he had trained himself to listen. Who told the myth to man? If you asked me that question let me ask you who told the mathematician to let x equal the value of a ton of hay. The mind of man is capable of thinking what it pleases and working out a great line of reasonings from its first premise.

All the Paul type have premised a cruel existence for the most worthy of men, and they have been such good logicians that they martyred themselves finally, just as logic from a terrible premise ought to do.

"What is the world but a mental presentation?" has been the question of thousands. What or who is Jesus Christ? He is the man that was and is and ever will be, like the plants that were before they were in the earth. He is man listening to his own soul. He is man turning to what is true of himself and ignoring the myth about himself.

Two Important Points

Paul here catches a glimpse again in the twenty-fourth verse: "None of these things move me, so that I might finish my course with joy." He who sees no danger mentions none. He who is joyous does not tell sorrowful things to wound loving hearts. Brave, worthy, hard-pressed Paul!

But he was not preaching the gospel of Jesus. He was only preaching that Jesus was Messiah. He believed in finishing his course with joy. These two points are all the attractions which any modern religion holds out to men. Jesus is Messiah or Savior, and we shall finish our course with joy. These two points have drawn the faithful hearts and brave services of multitudes. "Somewhere, sometime, we shall wear the crown and hear the plaudits," is their hope.

How is it that they wear the crown finally? Because every belief is temporary like the roses. It starts, it buds, it blooms, it falls. When the belief of the religionist has bloomed at its fullest it falls. Then the faithful religionist sees that it was a myth and shouts for delight at its freedom. Some wait for martyrdom, some wait for the grave, but that is because their premise journeyed that way. On their journey they often had foregleams (a dawning light) of freedom to come. This they called the final plaudit of effort. It was peace and freedom, health and rest for the future. But the gospel of Jesus is quite different. When he was asked when the kingdom of heaven should come he answered, "It is within you."

In the twenty-seventh verse the belief in hard and unremitting struggles to be worthy of peace is described at one of its halting places. The prophet Ezekiel is quoted as if wiser than Jesus. As one exulting commentator explains it, "Paul declared not only the premises of God, but his threatenings:

not only the pleasant and hopeful, but the terrible," and so was innocent of all neglect. "I am pure from the blood of all men." The Prophet Ezekiel said: "If thou warnest not the wicked he shall die in his iniquity, but his blood will I require at thy hands."

Truths of the Gospel

But Jesus said: "These things have I spoken unto you that ye might have peace," "Come unto me and I will give you rest." This is the gospel. The early church fastened the truth into the race mind that Jesus Christ has come. This truth will endure. They fastened another idea into it which even now is dissolving, viz., that we have to struggle as prisoners out of nets to become sons and daughters of God. Not being gospel it has bloomed as an idea on the world's sight in strenuous, Herculean exertions to be what we already were from the beginning and could not be any different if we should try for ages, and is now dropping away into "such lethargy on the part of dying souls as makes the heart of the good minister sad and fills the good God with righteous anger."

The premise of the so-called "dying souls" is no more misleading than that of the good minister; they both believe the Christian walk requires terrible strains and straits. One takes it in spite of his belief and the others refuse it because of their belief.

Paul spoke heroically of going "bound in spirit to Jerusalem." Nothing is so free as Spirit. The

Spirit binds nothing. The Spirit asks no bravery on my part or on your part. It does not bind anybody to do or not to do anything. It leaves all free as itself.

"I have not shunned to declare unto you all the counsel of God," said Paul. By reason of the premise he had taken, page after page of first joy and then sorrow to came rolling through his mind, and he read it off to his neighbors, just as he read it to himself, and believed in it all. This was to his credit. "Be not faithless but believing," is a good rule. It makes a warm heart, and active manner. But what do you believe? That is what rolls your daily lot past your eyes. Did you ever imagine that you would get into trouble by a certain event and after a few moments of thinking what a mistake you had made, get to trembling 'with fear or faint with discouragement. That premise you took rolled its logic swiftly around in your mind and acted itself outwardly.

Now take the premise that you have not got to struggle for another minute to be wise or powerful or safe from misfortune. Have the true God for your supreme confidence — the one who rains on the just and on the unjust alike, free from prejudice, free from partiality. It will take a great burden off your shoulders. You will feel wiser at once through freedom. You will feel more at peace through freedom. You will feel prosperous and the feeling will demonstrate in all things.

Kingdom of the Spirit

This is the counsel of God. You will not feel that there is any danger ahead of anybody. "There shall come among you grievous wolves," sorrowfully spoke Paul. To you there can be no wolves able to enter into anybody's lot. Such conditions are only the results of ideas. If anybody is strong enough to lug such heavy ideas they are strong enough to take the consequences of the ideas. This is what is meant by, "As thy day is so shall thy strength be." If your ideas have generated some little wolves you are quite able to bear their bites.

If people do not enjoy their "wolves," or more commonly speaking "trials," let them leave off root and branch from thinking according to Paul and the prophets and Adam. Who is there that can arise and throw off the old coat of believing that we are not all free spirit, as the blind man arose and ran after Jesus, casting his raiment behind him?

In our vested rights are we not as able to hurl the cyclone of truth through the circumambient mental atmospheres as the prophets and Adam were to hurl their groundless beliefs?

So psychologized was Paul with his thought of danger ahead for the church of Christ that he mournfully praised himself with the words: "I ceased not to warn every one night and day, with tears."

This little book, "The A.B.C. of the Way," tells how it happens that misfortunes come to the lot of man. Describing danger makes a strong magnet. Describe with tears and the magnet gets more potent. Keep at it day and night and the force will be powerful.

Describing the kingdom of spirit within — how does that magnify itself? Day and night keep on - with joyous increase of confidence in the truth that the kingdom of heaven is in all men alike now and awaits them ahead in their free future, and what kind of a world would you see?

Do Not Believe in Weakness

Have you known anybody who has practiced that way of managing his destiny and "laboring" for his fellow men?

You have known multitudes of faithful, brave Pauls, warning mankind of trial and misery, hades and Satan; have you known one — just one — who saw always the Spirit in man in its happy friendship, around him, ahead of him, with its glory of blessings indestructible?

Have you heard one tell day and night with the fidelity of the saints at their warnings about the unreality of Adam and his failure, his sickness and fear, his doubt and poverty, and the reality of freedom from sickness, fear, misfortune, with the good things laid up for us all from the beginning which belong to us now, and we could not get rid of if we wanted to, any more than we could be different from the beautiful and joyous spirit which God made us?

Do you think it a virtue to "support the weak," as this thirty-fifth verse of the twentieth chapter of Acts, now under our attention, tells us we must?

It is a virtue only because having believed in weakness we must of necessity support those who caught the results of our own belief. We must of necessity believe it is good to support our own offspring.

But who has shown how strong it is to be free from believing in weakness: In your own spirit you do not believe in weakness.

Inter Ocean Newspaper August 13, 1893

LESSON VIII

Conscious of a Lofty Purpose

Acts 21

Haydon wrote that Wordsworth and Keats were the only men he ever saw who looked conscious of a lofty purpose. Paul, the apostle, must have looked conscious of a lofty purpose. He lived and moved and had his being in the idea that he had been called to "come up to the help of the Lord against the mighty." While sitting at the feet of Gamaliel he became so moved with faith in the teachers of the law and the prophets whom Gamaliel interpreted to him, that he verily thought he was doing God service by persecuting the Christians.

Then on his way to Damascus the presence of Jesus Christ became visible to him and His voice spoke audibly that it was not of the spirit of God he had learned to scourge and imprison his fellow men. Immediately Paul gave up believing in attacking others for their religious views. But he did not give up believing in being attacked. His lofty purpose dropped off the old rag of men's opinions concerning persecution of people who did not believe his way, but kept to the last the tough but groundless leather conviction that not only is the way of the transgressor hard, but the way of the man in the right is harder.

Paul believed that the way of the Son of God is hardest of all. In this belief he is followed even to this day. We have churches built on the "persecuted, scourged, crucified Son of God". In a moment of supreme ascent out of the clutches of the world's opinion that the way of the Son of Omnipotence is harder than the way of the transgressor, Hicks, the Quaker, said; "To the Christ that never was crucified, to the Christ that never was buried, to the Christ that never arose, being forever arisen, unassailable glory, I commend you."

As a Son of God

His moment of inspired freedom spoke unalterable truth. The way of the son of God is the free spirit. Whoever lives as a son of God must live as free from misery and horror as the light of the world lives. "My peace give I unto you." "The peace that passeth understanding." To this free, unattached spirit, which is Son of God and God himself, there is a church founded. The members of this church have Paul's obedient spirit; they love his doctrine when he forgets to tell his private belief as the right one; they are never drawn for a second into the maelstrom of his subtle teaching that it is easier to be a transgressor than a son of God, for the "truth is now easier for them to believe than any man's *ipse dixit* (he himself said).

If we are in a certain state of mind we are sure to get information concerning things and events like it. While outside that state of mind we seek and work for the information, but it does not come. Paul's constant and abiding belief in the necessity for afflictions caused Agabus to tell him that if he went to Jerusalem to preach Jesus Christ, he would get violent maltreatment. If Paul had not been a powerful magnet to draw prophecies of evil, do you suppose poor Agabus could have made out the Holy Ghost to stand so helplessly by while its minister was preaching of its defense, support and strength? "He took Paul's girdle and bound his own hands and feet, and said, 'Thus saith the Holy Ghost, so shall the Jews at Jerusalem bind the man that owneth this girdle, and shall deliver him into the hands of the Gentiles'."

Then were the Christianized Jews all so tremblingly apprehensive that they advised Paul to forgo charges for four men to shave their heads and go through some external formulas and forms likely to conciliate those Jews who had heard that Paul was disreputable in certain respects.

Wherein Paul Failed

Here the good Paul, looking through the smoked glass of his own belief, lost the clear sight of the subtle principle whereby he was free to shave his head and scourge his body if he wished to, but he must understand that the ministry of the Spirit needs no helping along by shaving or not shaving.

"A poor old colored woman," as the neighbors were wont to speak of her, undertook to pray for a sick girl's recovery from chronic misery. She told the girl to lean wholly upon the praying and do nothing else whatsoever. Immediately the girl began to get well when the praying began. Her recovery was rapid. She ate and walked and slept better at once. She was free to eat what she pleased, walk as much as she pleased, sleep when she wanted to, but there came a day when she thought she would help the cure by eating regularly, walking just so-and-so, sleeping just so much, etc., then her progress toward recovery stopped. Do you see any reason for that stop? She was free to do what she pleased, providing she did not wrap the action in the swaddling leather of supposing that the Holy Ghost needed her help against the mighty disease that was fighting her.

When the so called ignorant washerwoman told her she must not "think de Lawd needed her assistance" she left off coming to his help and got well. "Why, I thought I was helping the Spirit! I thought it my duty to do everything I could to help it," the girl said. It is time the world knew that the Holy Governor of the universe is neither a tramp, a beggar nor a bankrupt, that he needs any help in exhibiting life, health, strength, support and defense wherever his Truth is spoken.

"Cast all your care on God!

That anchor holds.

Is He not yonder in the uttermost of the seas?

The sea is his, he made it."

You may have the shining countenance of a lofty purpose, but you will get banged around and defeated with violent oppositions often and much, just as the church founded on the same proposition has, if you keep for an idea that you must come up to the help of the Lord against the mighty, whether it be to destroy the so-called "mighty" sickness that seems to be wasting you, the cause for grief that chases you around, or the poverty in one or other phase that stays in your house.

Must Give Up the Idea.

I am free to go to Europe or Africa. I am free to climb the Himalayas or starve myself in Malta, but I shall have to stay there hindered and mobbed like Paul, hindered and sickened like the young girl, or utterly routed like Uzza (see I Chron. 8:9), if I think I can advance the church I belong to, the school I represent, the doctrine of Jesus or the demonstrations of the Almighty Spirit of God by any of these undertakings.

"What must I do? Just what the girl did. Give up my idea of assisting the Holy Ghost. The moment I give up that unprofitable mental luggage I see my way clear to prosperity in demonstration.

"Seven" is a number consecrated to fulfillment of law as "three" is a number consecrated to answered prayer, and "forty" is by some commentators said to be consecrated to affliction. Paul undertook to go through the Jewish forms, but his understanding of their worthlessness in themselves bore down so hard upon his imagination that they might conciliate the Jews and facilitate his ministry that, before the seven days essential to proof of such efficacy were completed, he was seized by the mob.

They who cling to the law watch the seven days' progress through. They who accept the gospel through working in the law get along very well for a while and then have a rough time of it. Paul still held to Jewish customs after he had agreed with the Christian freedom.

Paul also had confidence in his doctrine sufficiently strong to think that when preached it would convert people. Feeling that he had a call from the Omnipotent to preach, he had a saving clause in his mind always which lifted him out of every scrape he got into. He was like a ship that rides the waves, dipping low to demonstrate a false idea, lifting high to demonstrate a true idea, never gliding swiftly over smooth waters to demonstrate one changeless principle.

Associated with Publicans

"Trophimus" was considered bad company for a first-class Jew to be associated with. Paul had the Jesus Christ principle here, for he never considered anybody bad company who had evinced honest faith in his doctrine. Therefore he associated with "Trophimus," and like poor Tray, his bad company was blamed for what was only his own fault.

"When Jesus Christ was giving an object lesson in the way a false idea leads you and me into complications he got into a position where they said that he associated "with publicans and sinners",

The science of Christianity is very upsetting to old beliefs. Take this one about keeping good company, for instance. Those who are called bad company very seldom think other people are sinners; they blame themselves. Those who are called good company pull away their skirts with pale-faced horror from those others, because they think themselves very good and the others very bad. If there is any choice as to which set is the most wholesome to associate with it is that set which feels that itself needs the purifying and accepts the teaching that keeps its adherents repeating formulas which are self-purifying. Self-righteous people are really the greatest believers in evil, for they believe the atmosphere around them, is very bad, while the so-called sinners believe the atmosphere around them is better than they are. "Trophimus" thought the Jews were divine. He believed the Christians were very good. He thought he himself needed much formula to keep decent. It is the belief of people in what is outside of them that we breathe when we associate with them. It makes their atmosphere. Of course in spiritual science no degrees or choices of evil are admitted, but if there were any choice we could easily see why Jesus Christ loved the atmosphere of the sinners so well.

While "Trophimus" was loving and admiring his neighbors they were traducing (slandering) him. Many other foolish suppositions beside those mentioned in this Acts 21 are going to fall away from all minds. This chapter hints at them, and in other chapters they are plainly visible. One is that the people we think are opposing us are really doing us good, and we had better give them room to exercise their oppositions in. The Jews thought Paul was opposed to their best interests while he was working for them. It was his own idea that they caught concerning themselves.

He thought before he arrived among them that they were against him. He was very powerful with his ideas, indeed so powerful that a whole mob caught every one he had. When he thought of healing, they all screamed with delight that they were healed. When he thought of mobs they all rose like puppets to become mobs. "Trophimus" had not such vigorous strength in his ideas. If he had had the crowd would have been very happy when he thought of them as happy. They held him lightly because he held himself lightly. You must according to mental science, expect to see your own ideas and feelings expressed by those you meet.

Rights of the Spirit

There is a startling proposition right here. Paul felt that being "a Jew of Tarsus" he had supreme right to be heard. Do you look upon yourself as having some mighty rights for some particular reason? That is a sign you have the rights and may have the opportunities and privileges that go with them, but you must say it is for any other reason than that you are an advocate of irresistible spirit, born of spirit, exercising every privilege because you are spirit, that you expect to manage the hindrance to your prosperity.

You need not think that giving as a reason for your expectation of success that you are rich or talented, or backed up by great people, or youth or beauty or brilliant intellect will bring the requisite flavor of satisfaction. Such reasons are temporary expedients; they are lame feet; they exasperate the mob while you give voice to your sentiments or keep silent with respect to them. Paul's description of himself as "a citizen of no mean city" just got a little temporal breath of opportunity. It did not save him from being taken into the castle bound with new thongs. There is only one reason why you should have the right of a happy prosperous way through this universe, and that is because from God you came forth, of God you are made, through God is your journey, to God you go.

And in giving this reason for your unquestioned nobility, wisdom, and greatness, all the mobs of the earth are convinced that you are right, because they see that what is true of you is true of themselves. "Let him that boasteth, boast in the God of Truth." He who speaks of an advantage or disadvantage over his fellow men, or under them, will hear the crowds cry as Paul did, "Away with him." He who even thinks in his heart that he has any advantage over or disadvantage under his fellow beings, need not be surprised at being held to new trials, for thoughts will externalize. There is in Truth no advantage or disadvantage. We are all one.

Inter Ocean Newspaper August 20, 1893

LESSON IX

Measure of Understanding

Acts 26:19-32

The Christian doctrine accomplishes two results upon those who receive it. The measure of their results is the measure of their understanding. They who receive it are lifted out of sin and sickness just as far as they admit that the doctrine can lift them out of such delusions, and being once free they are kept free, for "the prayer of faith shall save the sick," and "God is able to make him stand."

Paul had accepted enough Christian doctrine to make him unflinchingly fearless, and he demonstrated distinctly for all time to note exactly how much of the doctrine he understood. As beliefs formulate after awhile by marching sets of conditions round us, so Paul's peculiar ideas on certain questions took him from captivity under Felix and Drusilla, the happy and youthful, to captivity under Festus and Bernice, the joyous and victorious. Every name is significant of character, as it is meant to be. The unit one looks to ciphers at its right and sees ascending values; to left and sees descending values, so the name of a child is not given him accidentally. Causes led up to it as rightly expressing his formulation. It is his unit. He does with it what he pleases when he meets the world with it. If he deals with descending ideas he must meet descents of conditions, if with lofty thoughts then with noble surroundings.

Felix means happy, but Felix was not happy. Festus means joyous, but history makes Festus out a cynic and skeptic. A name stands for what ways it is easiest for the child to look. Easily Festus might have been joyous, easily he was cynical. Time has not changed in signifying what two ways are easiest for a child to look, to right or left with his thoughts.

It was a long imprisonment for Paul in Caesarea. He was detained there two years. He was exceedingly wise in every move he made and every word he spoke while there. By his courtesy and intelligence he caused King Agrippa to exclaim: "Almost thou persuaded me to be a Christian." He got King Agrippa and Governor Festus to see that he had a right to liberty exactly as he had convinced Felix and Tertullus of the same.

Lesser of Two Evils

By appealing to Caesar they were obliged to detain him. Thus he had the liberty of a respected captive. Really it was of two evils the less, for the

Jews were lying in wait outside to make away with him the instant he should show himself. The adroitness and skill with which Paul spake and acted so as to be safe, and respected while imprisoned are evidence of how easy it was for him to think spiritually.

The spirit will work wonderfully to help people to get out of complications and dangers. It is an ever ready power. It never reproves a man for getting into tight places, by his mistakes. It takes every situation just as it finds it, and has some skillful way out, so that nobody ever need think he has offended the spirit or got out of the range of its help. There is for the very worst of us a vision or a dream, or an inspiration or a friendly direction, or constantly recurring motto or scripture text, or memory that tells us how to be free. The spirit is God. It works toward what will be for our peace, prosperity, and protection. Thus it held Paul within the castle walls till he could hear its directing words, which, the moment he heard and spoke them, would be his freedom.

Now, at the opening of this lesson, he is explaining himself to his captors. Agrippa means one who has caused pain, or can cause great peace. It is difficult to turn the tongue or the heart of one who loves to speak sarcastically, or who keeps twitting of faults, so, in watching the world from the standpoint of the one who is twitted, it became consistent with feeling and experience for some mothers to name their boys Agrippa. For such characters there is only one way to reach them, and that is through talk and description of spiritual things. They are always thirsty for talk on spiritual themes.

Ever after Paul's address before Agrippa that king held a kindly feeling for the Nazarenes. At the time of the great Jewish war, some eight or nine years after this scene at Caesarea, he protected the Christians.

Festus also was much moved to friendly feeling for Paul. He wrote such a letter to Nero, Emperor of Rome (Caesar), that he was acquitted and set free. Since every man and woman whom we meet personifies some undercurrent of thought we hold, some speech or writing we have perpetually indulged in, so also Festus certainly was manifesting Paul's accusing tendency. He called Paul crazy, just as Paul had always felt that everybody was insane who opposed him in an argument or differed from him in the slightest.

A Conciliating Spirit

Bernice, also, when we read her history, is plainly Paul's own quality standing distinctly out. Paul thought a great deal on these subjects which she represented. As truly and spiritually no man or woman is what we call him or what he looks to be as flesh, we may find out our errors by taking an inventory of our associates whose looks or conduct we are not pleased with.

This lesson breathes a powerfully conciliating spirit. It would be a good scripture section to read over several times if people have got the advantage of you in any way, for it will insinuate through their thoughts the rights of your case. (Acts 26:19-32)

One student of such scripture sections as convey special qualities, always holds his breath while reading them or scarcely breathes, in order that the texts may have full sway with him. Another breathes deeply and rapidly while reading important and powerful passages. These students have heard the Shinto doctrines taught, explaining how, as we breathe, we inhale and expel the thoughts of our heart as we do the atmosphere.

Others think that either of these processes is a material performance for a spiritual result, and they can scarcely conceal their contempt of such materially minded people. Paul's conciliatory mind, while not giving up a single proposition of his wonderful religion, will thus be a great treatment for such as feel contempt of their neighbors, for he caused contempt and pride to fall away from some very powerful people, according to this lesson.

It begins with the words, "Whereupon, O! King Agrippa, I was not disobedient unto the heavenly vision." All the success and power of Paul's warfare may be charged to his changeless fidelity to this one vision. He often forgot his other less violent visions, and we cannot help wondering why he expected so much pain and defeat when the Lord Jesus Christ spoke audibly to him so often, promising him peace and protection, but this one never slipped away from him. Its information he never disputed. To us there can be no doubt of his historic adventures with their spiritual significations being intended for us to see plainly that, if every vision had commanded his obedience as this one did he would not have marked his Christian journey with imprisonments and bloodshed.

Paul, in common with centuries of Christians under the sway of his views, believed that following the Lord Jesus Christ meant taking his apparent experiences. Peter even begged for crucifixion. Paul said they all preferred death rather than life.

Was fellowship with death the doctrine of Jesus?

A Dream of Uplifting

Those who see plainly that Jesus was teaching how to demonstrate peace in the midst of turmoil, do not think they are very Christlike if they are still mixed with turmoil. They do not urge that it was his proposition to sanctify them by sickness, but to take them out of sickness. They find that their gentle and unostentatious visions of direction are as much to be obeyed as the strong and violent ones. If they open to a scripture passage which touches their case they call that a heavenly vision and follow it obediently as much as if an angel had appeared to them and promised them direction and guidance. The often-turning to one idea as they turn over the leaves of their Bible, is a heavenly vision to them if they believe its purport.

A dream of uplifting is to be remembered and trusted if Paul's life is worth anything. If it seems impossible for your prophetic Bible verse to be fulfilled in you, all the more should you believe it, for the seemingly impossible is the easiest possible for the spirit. Did it not seem an impossibility for a regiment of soldiers to fall as if shot at the sight of the countenance of one man? Yet they fell. So can the horrors of your hardships "fold their tents and steal away" at the touch of the spirit you believe in, whose promise was given you too gently for you to confide in?

Paul says that he went forward immediately and preached repentance and works meet for repentance after that vision. He felt the need of promptly relieving men of their present modes of belief. They were all sinners and needed to repent and work like saints. He repented himself and set forth to be a martyr. He was gloriously consistent in this, not asking of his neighbors what he did not undertake himself, and never saving them any scotching he felt it their duty to take. He was merciless with himself and with everybody else because he believed this to be the doctrine of Jesus. Whatever peace they got they must look forward to another realm for this one was all contention.

We have found the spiritual import of these lessons often denying this doctrine of pain and terror. It is not wise or truthful to teach children that there is a God in heaven ordaining the principle of evil to have place in his world. The wisdom is in teaching them that the good is the ruling principle, nothing can defeat it.

The Highest Endeavor

The truth to tell children about themselves is not that they are sinful, but that they have a spiritual principle within them which cannot be defeated, will not feel pain. Never fails in anything. Their highest endeavor shall be to be entirely one with that irresistible principle. This spiritual principle is now kept by us all more or less in the region of the subconscious mind because the conscious mind is devoted to thinking how to earn a living, get along with neighbors, or hold our own among our various relations. It is from this region that the light shines into the atmosphere and formulates visions. It is this that points out to us the scripture text that is meant to be our intelligence.

Its mission is to be an array with banners under a mighty general acting forever in our behalf. If we look slightingly upon the meager threads of help it throws out, we will hide the coming threads. These are heavenly visions. We need not complain of them, for they were all we permitted to appear. It is no fault of the army of helpers within us that we get so little help. They give us all we will let them give.

Can you not see how in Paul's case he had slight need to slight appearances? But the slightest film blowing in the wind shows its direction. Paul had enough doctrine on the unreality of matter and the absoluteness of Spirit to have saved his world. He believed the Spirit had all power and there was nothing beside it. This doctrine was itself a heavenly vision. Did he believe the Spirit voluntarily led Christians into hardships? Do you believe that? The true doctrine as a heavenly vision has no such proposition.

Paul insisted that "we wrestle against spiritual wickedness in high places". This is giving a dignity to wickedness which truth does not give it. "I never preached anything only what the prophets and Moses did say should come — that Christ should suffer," said Paul. But the prophets and Moses told two sets of ideas; sometimes they looked to the right of their unit and sometimes to the left. Faithful Paul followed their veerings. "They shall not hurt or kill in all my holy mountain," "A man's word is his only burden," "There is only God," they said. If after that they told of misery and death, was it necessary to follow them down that track?

Paul at Caesarea

There is no sweeter courtesy of conduct or faithfulness of speech on the side of the reality and dominion of a spiritual principle or power than

Paul's at Caesarea while a prisoner. He never referred to his healing power as an evidence of his Christianity, and never made the entire peace and safety of an apostle a sign of right faith. He confined his discourses to descriptions of Jesus Christ. This theme in itself bore constantly toward fulfilling his highest hopes.

Though the disciples and apostles all healed, they said very much less about its being an evidence of Christianity than Jesus Christ himself had said.

They all felt most imbued with the one mission of informing the world that the prophesied Messiah had already appeared on the earth. The multitudes did not know that scripture had been so far fulfilled. They must be told. They were told well. Great numbers were convinced that Jesus of Nazareth was the personified Christ who was coming again though he had disappeared for that period. They practiced throwing their thoughts upon him till their faces shone with angelic light. His particular teachings they paid very little attention to. They hid the finest promises he made by the dark belief in their call to pain and starvation. They looked ahead toward his second coming for the peace and protection his doctrine should give instantly. His coming again was to be really according to his own words more as a right teaching than as a man among men, and they hid their sight of him by looking to his personality rather than to his principles, which are his second coming.

Healing is the first evidence of spiritual light. It is the key to all demonstration. The man who is perfectly healthy has no faults of character. Dishonesty, backbiting, greed, intemperance are diseases. The healthy man does not have them. According to Jesus Christ to be healthy was the first evidence of spiritual birth.

How did he regard disease? He regarded it as a delusion. No matter whether it were the disease of poverty or palsy, it was a delusion. He had great power over delusions.

Paul proclaimed that "Christ should show light unto the people and to the gentiles." If a lily looks black in the night it is a delusion which the light will clear up. All through the scriptures of nations "light" is the symbol of truth and understanding. Show men what is true and you show them the light. So eagerly have people sought for truth that they have worshipped every symbol of it. The sun, moon, and stars have been adored. Water, fresh from the wells, set in the sunshine till every circle thereof had been swathed in splendor, must be drunk the first thing every morning. They practiced eating alone in the sun, sleeping alone to watch for the morning, and solitary communion with the sunshine. They prostrated themselves before the dawning light and praised its glory. They shouted at high noon, and at evening they recounted its mercies.

Preparatory Symbols

These were all preparatory symbols of the light that Jesus brought. The preaching of the power of Jesus Christ to raise from the dead as Paul gave it was still in the realm of symbol, because he made death such a real and substantial process. It was a coming sure event for all men. If it were very violent and cruel it were all the more Godlike. He did not teach that the doctrine of Jesus could annul the process.

Jesus Christ made everything the product of words. False words were dead words — nothing to them. This was death. True words were life — solid substance. Being full of true words, any mind would be healthy. Its body would be healthy. Its actions would be healthy. What these true words were should be known plainly. There should the end be.

"All the host of heaven shall be dissolved, and the heavens shall be rolled together as a scroll; and all their host shall fall down as the leaf falleth from the vine, and as a falling fig from the tree."

This is rapidly transpiring now. Then all the poor shall hear what Jesus Christ meant by preaching a gospel to them. His gospel shakes the great ones as it bloweth where it listeth through the upper airs, and their money, their fields, their ships, must pass into hands with just hearts controlling them. No man can withhold more than is meet when the wind of the right gospel blowing on the word from the high doctrine of Christ is even thought in one heart.

What is his doctrine concerning imprisonment? "I set the captive free, I open prison doors." What is his doctrine concerning sorrow and mourning? "I bring the oil of joy for mourning." What is his doctrine concerning poverty? "I preach the gospel to the poor. Riches are with me, yea, durable riches. I feed the hungry, clothe the naked." What is his doctrine to the overburdened? "I bring the garment of praise for the spirit of heaviness. My kingdom is an everlasting kingdom."

Who is there ready while poverty seems real in his sight to say, "I do not believe in poverty?" Who is there ready while dangers seem flying toward him to say, "I do not believe in danger?" Who is there ready while seemingly fainting under his burden of human existence to say, "I believe only in freedom?"

Do you suppose such a statement of faith shall fly unheeded?

Evidences of Christianity

Paul turned to Agrippa and said: "I would to God that not only thou, but also all that hear me this day were both almost, and altogether such as I am, except, these bonds." What made those bonds? He made them himself, for he believed in bonds.

If a Christian today is free from handcuffs and ankle chains, but still wears the collar of indebtedness or sickness, he has only shifted his belief a little from Paul's position; he still needs a draught from the doctrine of Jesus. At his highest point of preaching he must still secretly be saying, "except these bonds" for he still believes in bonds.

If one preaches of the peace of this doctrine, who is still wrought up over his affairs, he is tacitly saying, "except these bonds". If one preaches of the power of the gospel to set free from fleshly appetites who still demands a particular way of living as essential to his comfort, he is plainly saying, "except these bonds". It is no use trying to make out that the perfect doctrine is honestly believed in while we, like Paul, can point to our ankle chains and handcuffs which show that we are the victims of our past thoughts on their down grade. Freedom, prosperity, health, vigor, fearless, tireless energy, with nobody before whom to plead our cause, to carry our points, but only a crowd of glad listeners to the message that the way of the martyr, the way of the sick, the way of bloodshed are not the pathway of the true believer. This is evidence of Christianity. This is not condemnation of the martyrs, but only understanding them in the light as the lily is seen when morning has come.

The crowned heads who listened to Paul said he had done nothing worthy of death, and they gave him safe escort to Rome, where it had been his choicest wish to go.

Thus Paul confronted his down-grade thoughts in Festus, Agrippa, and Bernice, and by drinking of the distilled doctrine of safety in small draughts, turned to his upgrade thoughts sufficiently to be respectfully regarded and helped as much as he could have been helped without another miracle. The same doctrine is able, if taken in full measure, to keep whoever drinks of it from ever compelling any son of God to appear in the light of victory to turn to the captor's side to be won over to the captive's cause, or as joy showing its cynical opposite to be healed by a joyful message, as Paul by his discourses had compelled Festus and Bernice. For, "the Lord is able to make thee stand" if thou receive him into an un-sicklied mind, though he is able to heal thee if thou hast made thyself sick.

Inter Ocean Newspaper August 27, 1893

LESSON X

The Angels of Paul

Acts 27

Festus committed Paul into the hands of Julius, the captain of the Roman guard, to convey him by ship from Caesarea to Rome. The ship was wrecked on the coast of Malta. Paul had advised them not to sail at the time they were set upon launching, but they paid no heed to his advice and were all in great danger of being drowned when an angel from heaven appeared unto Paul in the midst of his earnest praying and promised him that not only he but all on board should be saved.

Paul's thoughts must have been very noble and pure to have personified themselves so often in beautiful angels. If our nights are terrified by uncanny dreams or strange unwholesome beings, we may see that we are filled with low bred notions during our days, and not glorified meditations. After his promise Paul saw the sailors letting down the lifeboat to save themselves "under color as though they would cast anchor." Paul felt the impulse to exclaim, "Except these abide in the ship, ye cannot be saved." If the sailors had been forced to leave the ship, the company would have been saved. If the officers had weakly permitted them to run away from their duty they would simply have refused their offer of life.

To this day people have prophetic visions of assistance, and then, like Paul, instinctively put out their protests when something threatens to upset the fulfillment of the promise.

Paul seemed to speak too impulsively to be responsible for his speech. That which is done from kindly impulse cannot be considered as indicative of distrust of any principle by onlookers, though Paul's speech sounded much against the angel's promise, that no matter what happened, not a soul on board should be hurt.

We are inclined to be telling ourselves, and our children that if we do not do so and something bad will happen, and if we do thus or thus we shall surely come to grief. It is the continual cropping out of that streak of fearfulness which we are all accused of having.

It is the signal of great faith if you have come to where you are never heard saying that if you throw yourself down from the mountain you surely will be hurt, or stand in a draught you surely will be sick. Jesus did not do any violence to himself. But he did not give as a reason for saving himself that he was afraid of being hurt. "Thou shalt not tempt the law of safety," he said.

Paul's Source of Inspiration

Therefore, Paul has been called unscientific for threatening harm where an angel had said there could be none. He used language which would appeal to the officers, and succeeded. He is noted for ability to be all things to all men, and to put themselves into their understanding readily.

Julius admired and loved him, and the whole crew believed him when he told them that the spirit had promised they should come safely to land; He shows to the best advantage in this shipwreck of anywhere he is described. His lofty calm and motherly tenderness are driving against the dark background of raging sea and gloomy howls of Euroclydon (a cyclonic tempestuous northeast wind).

Paul had a mighty genius for praying. Over and again he was answered by miracles. Here he abstained from food and from speech for a long time, as it reads to identify, himself entirely, with his prayers. If you read over his life at Ephesus you feel the genius for healing stir in you. If you read over his life at Corinth, you feel the presence of the Holy Ghost. If you read over his history through imprisonments and shipwrecks you catch his inspiration in prayer. The first thing you notice will be that he does not plead with a being to help him, he speaks firmly and confidently as to a friend who is sure to help, and yet he does not give over telling the friend what he wants, till the friend says, "I will help you."

He has no time to eat, drink or talk while he is holding interview with the Almighty. The rest of us eat, drink, and discuss affairs while we are intermittently talking with the divine spirit. (Acts 27:21) The second hint we get of the law of prevailing prayer is that our very spiritual nature waits for us to tell it what to do and how to do it. Suppose I cry like Daniel, "O Lord hear; O Lord, forgive; O Lord, harken and do; defer not" — it is not expected of that Lord within my being that I shall cringe and fear at its feet, but that I shall tell definitely what I want it to hear and what I want done.

Its forgiveness is its power to take the other ideas out of my mind except the one idea for which I have come into its presence.

Every prayer that is recorded as having been answered has been noticed being full of affirmation of what the Lord is able to do and what it will do. "Thou art my redeemer." "Stretch forth thine arm to help me now." The willing spiritual nature moves to listen. If we are in great misery we turn off from thinking of help and sure mercy and maunder and whine feel as well as to eat and sleep is what we discover Paul's abstinence consisted in.

Should Not Be Miserable

The temptation to howl and talk and think about our troubles is as much our meat and drink as the beefsteak and coffee of our breakfast. Our mind would be quite hungry if it did not have a misery to lament over. Just notice how as soon as the great cause of our mourning is past we find another little cause for complaining, and talk, and meditate on that one till it is very large in our sight.

Now to abstain from mourning over any trouble, or talking it over or being half-witted or face paled because of it is abstinence. Paul could do this, but he had to stop eating and sleeping and talking while he told the spirit which was so free and fearless just how free he wished the ship's company to be.

In times of overpowering trouble the spirit is the only helper. Then we abstain from looking to mankind or material props. Many people have seen miraculous deliverances, when terribly hard pushed, who could not see them when hard beset by daily annoyances. Total abstinence is as necessary for daily trials as for shipwrecks according to this lesson.

The soldiers were taking other prisoners besides Paul to Rome to be tried for various offenses, with the hope they might escape death. Escape was their desire. When the soldiers discovered that the prisoners might escape from the broken boat they started to slay them. This is something like the weeping of Great Britain over the loss of the Victoria's crew2. She had lifted them out to kill and be killed, but when they were killed she tore her name with grief. Sometimes the law works things out very literally. The intended victims of the soldiers of the Victoria warship had somebody in their midst with a mind capable of protecting a multitude.

If the Victoria's crew had met them in battle they would have defeated her guns and made quick work of her men. But this mind never let her meet them in battle.

Better to Prevent than Cure

On this principle of the defense beforehand which a strong mind is for its comrades it has been seen that it is not needful to prepare for disaster, for none can come where that mind is. We shall not need surgeons for a community where one is spiritually vigorous enough to prevent the entrance of sickness into his township. We shall need armies where one can stop a Victoria from entering his country's ports or cause a regiment to refuse to fight his people.

It is better to prevent happenings than to cure them. Paul prevented very little, but he cured immense situations. His presence saved the life of the other prisoners, but did not smooth the seas. It is all smooth sailing and there are no lives to be saved where the spirit is perfectly manifest. Life is not in danger, for "where the spirit of Christ is there is liberty."

Julius kept custody of Paul, but though it was protracted imprisonment for Paul. Julius was not culpable. He had been ordered by Agrippa and Festus to keep hold of him to the last moment for the Roman government, would discover his character and believe him a good man, and their judgment would be found right.

When the wreck set Paul free he would not desert the shipwrecked crew, but helped to feed and warm them, as if he had been a hired helper, or an owner of the boat. Some of them swam safely to land and some clung to boards and floated shoreward. All escaped drowning. Paul's prayer saved them all. "They which could swim cast themselves first into the sea and got to land, and the rest, some on broken boards and some on pieces of the ship. And so it came to pass that they escaped all safe to land."

So by the presence of the spirit are some able to be quickly healed and others to be slowly healed, but the spirit never fails to bring them all to shore where there is one among them to pray with the concentrated energy of Paul.

Mysteries of Providence

There is a great lesson of the mysteries of Providence in the way those 300 people were fed. Leaning entirely upon the spirit Paul got the islanders to urge the crew to take away provisions on their further voyaging. Had Paul leaned on the islanders themselves they would not have furnished anything.

If any among us has been leaning on his houses, lands, and bank stocks he has found what feeble props they make for times of financial shipwreck. Suddenly they are worthless as security for dollars. But if he has been leaning on the spirit of God he has not found any lack of dollars or opportunities. In the panic of the capitalists the hand of the spiritually minded is plainly discovered. Their knowledge that opportunities and money should be equally distributed, and that in the life of the spirit which moves through our midst there is no rich and no poor, no burdened and no exempt in contradistinction, has been potent to shake their trees of possessions for the benefit of others. The shaking is so hard and shall be so further hard that the true prop to lean upon shall come plainly into sight of all mankind as the one only principle by which to live.

Those who cling to the spirit shall not know want. They shall not fail or fade or fear. By one way and another, on boats or by swimming, they shall all land safely, and those who represent the islanders of this lesson shall house and feed them bountifully. The spiritual principle of one in our midst shall stop the onward march of such enemies as the crew of the Victoria were preparing to be to some foreign navy, and open the hearts of some otherwise savage inhabitants of the strange shores upon which we have come in these times. Of a surety we know that we have the spirit of Christ here among us, and where that is there is liberty.

Inter Ocean Newspaper, September 3, 1893

LESSON XI

The Hope of Israel

Acts 28:20-31

There are two ways of being reduced to absolute nothingness, or that state where we all belong. One is by the experiences which transpire in our daily lot, and the other is by scientific acceptance of the right of doctrine. Every crushing or humiliating circumstance, every sarcasm, every misfortune, every battlefield or railway disaster is only the struggle of the external world to be lost in the internal world which is the nothing, or nothing. The moment that you see the sharp tongue of your neighbor or the rough action of your brother is your natural way of being uncovered of the rags of delusion you do not suffer pain of mind at them.

Paul opened this lesson by saying: "For the hope of Israel I am bound with this chain." "The hope of Israel" was the Messiah. The more binding and scourging those got who were killed with the Messiah, of course the more exposed the Messiah became. The early Church had a motto that "the blood of the martyrs is the see of the church." So pleased were they all with this way of being made a church that they quite ignored the other way of taking off dust particles from the spirit of pure doctrine, viz. by entering at once into doctrine itself, and having no experiences to tell of as to the steps by which they got there.

Immunity for Disciples

There is no question but that there is absolute immunity from history for those who become the doctrine of Jesus. They have no prisons to record; no sword cuts of body or mind to write about. Paul had times of immunity from hurts. He had then no history of pain to make mile-stones for his after hearers. Here at Rome, "living in his own hired house," he preached the kingdom of God, with all confidence, no man forbidding him." While he was talking with people who believed that suffering is the best way to get unformulated, he pointed to his chains as a sign that he was obedient to regular opinion. The next Paul, representative of the truth of Jesus, not the imaginary conception thereof, will not knuckle to opinion. He will be free from the outset of his recognition of the Messiah.

Opinions are a clog in the mind's onward flow. All the pressure of right doctrine put against them does not drive them out if held by the will, and all suffering that comes is only mind holding hard to opinions, while truth is pressing against the closed throttle valve. Will an engine stir if there is no vent for the steam? Will a fire burn if there is no draught? Will a mind move if mighty ideas are held back of opinions?

Therefore give up opinions, your own and those of the world. One set of opinions you are clogged with which, as this lesson expresses it has waxed your ears gross so that you can not hear, and closed your eyes so that you can not see when the truth is presented, is that you are often mistaken, often sinful, often foolish and often ignorant. This is quite a clog.

Hiding Inferiorities

There are two ways of getting unclogged of your secretly kept feelings that you do wish you knew more and did not make such blunders. If you have been trying to hide your inferiorities under the cloak of making believe that you were quite wise, or quite good, while you felt quite the opposite, or while you were trying to make yourself believe you were of some consequence, and would not face up your secret feeling that you were a humbug, it is your clearing out modus operandi to pour out the whole bottled mass into the Messiah's presence by confessing yourself a miserable, ignorant, foolish sinner. Pour out your confession hard. As the Messiah, or the perfect doctrine, has the idea that you are sinless wisdom, of course it is opening the throttle valve of your mind to pour out your secret opinions and let the true doctrine flow through.

This explains why "confession of sin" is so "good for the soul" according to Paul, though he did not explain it this way.

We were all "born in sin" and "conceived in iniquity" so we are told, which only means that we came among a host of people holding opinions, and we accepted pretty nearly all of them from the first breath. As that is our belief in secret, while we are trying to plaster over with efforts to be good in spite of our "inwardness," a good, free, full confession is a perfect relief. Every confession Paul made was followed by great freedom and great accomplishments. "For the hope of Israel I am bound with these chains," he said. There he converted Seneca, the tutor of Nero, who lived in history as famed as Paul. He convinced the Roma soldiers, who took turns in binding him under surveillance, that Jesus was Christ and they carried his teachings to England.

Pure Principle

If Paul held opinions like his church concerning sin and bondage his one way of opening the draught thus clogged was by confessing his opinions. If he saw himself as Jesus Christ saw him he had no confession to make and therefore no pain to undergo in becoming the pure doctrine, which is unopinioned principle.

Pure principle cannot be bound. They who let pure principle speak, write, and think through them live always free from trouble, sickness, fear, pain. The mere presence of trouble is sign of time for confession of internal clogs in the beliefs in our unworthiness. To pour out our beliefs on the bosom of unformulated principle is to give it a chance to pour its idea into the vacuum. We cannot make goodness see badness. Confessing our beliefs to the eternal understanding here near us does not convince it of our wickedness. We see ourselves as it sees us by such confession. Daniel, who was so free from accepting the opinions of the powerful Chaldeans that he could work miracles, still had so much Jewish opinion of sinfulness left in him that he could not understand his dreams or converse with angels till he had humbly fallen before his God as a burdened and imprisoned sinner exactly as Paul had to from having accepted the same teachings.

"And while I was speaking and praying and confessing my sins yea, while I was speaking in prayer, even the man Gabriel, whom I had seen in the vision in the beginning, being caused to fly swiftly, touched me and said, 'O, Daniel I am come to give thee skill and understanding. I am come to thee for thou art greatly beloved. Then Daniel was wise and free. He wrought miracles."

The whole purport of this twentieth to thirty-first of Acts twenty-eighth, is to show how humble delivery of our secret opinions will give free play for truth.

"O Lord! I have believed badly about myself. My heart is full of self-depreciation. Take thou my sinfulness and see me thine own way and work thine own will with me."

Inter Ocean Newspaper, September 10, 1893

LESSON XII

Joy in the Holy Ghost

Romans 14

The golden text of this lesson is, "It is good neither to drink wine, nor anything whereby thy brother stumbleth." The two texts which stand out in explanation of all the rest and which call for the ideal principle of life are:

1. *"There is nothing unclean of itself; but to him that esteemeth anything to be unclean, to him it is unclean."*

2. *"For the kingdom of God is not meat and drink; but joy in the Holy Ghost."*

As usual the closing quarterly lesson is called a temperance study, and as usual The International Committee handle it from the standpoint of phenomenal or apparent conduct of mankind making out that drinking rum, eating opium and gambling with their accompaniments are in themselves more powerful than the generality of mankind, and that man must stop conducting himself in company with these things or die. The golden texts hints hard that some men are exceedingly weak and that their stronger brethren must comport themselves in a deceitful manner to strengthen them. Its furthest insinuation is that the temperance lecturer may take a glass or two behind the door, where no neighbor with a weaker will than his can see him, and we all know that Paul took wine when no natural-born drunkards could be tempted by seeing him. In this again, Paul is honorably consistent.

The Ideal Doctrine

An ideal can be pushed to its extremest interpretation. It is the ideal doctrine which proclaims that "there is nothing unclean in itself, but to him that esteemeth anything to be unclean." It applies to man himself and the will of man also. Push it on its noblest proclamation. Surely it means that man himself is not a creature of appetite except to him that esteemeth him to be such, and to him he will continue to appear a creature of appetites till the esteemer changes his estimation. Man is not a being of weak will except to him whose mind judgeth him that way. Paul, therefore, rises to an ideal proposition in the thirteenth verse of his sermon to the Romans (chapter xiv.), where he says: "Let us not, therefore, judge one another anymore." He feels, away back there in the city of merchandise and appetite, that there is a high and glorious way to regard those people of Corinth who so sorely tempt him to believe in the reality of the material sense. He writes from that standpoint in brilliant spiritual axioms, and then remembering how real the boozy native's conduct seems, he talks of temporizing and outwardly appearing in order to wheedle them by the hook or crook somehow into the kingdom of heaven.

At the first glance it would seem that the ideal doctrine concerning man would upset the world, for it announces that if I see or deal with drunkards, I myself am dead drunk, with false estimations of the people I dwell among, not one of them being in any sense intoxicated with anything and having no appetite or weakness of will leading him into the snares of temptation in any way.

It is said in prophecy that when the third angel shall sound a star falls from heaven burning as it were a lamp but it acteth as wormwood to many men so that they die. The third angel is the message from high concerning the true nature of man. Its wormwood is its bitterness to the opinion held by church and state and school as to man's duty with man.

Tells a Different Story

Have they not held that man is an ignoramus with conserved potentialities of ability if trained to know matter well? But the loftiest star that drops from the heavens, taking majestic possession of man, tells a different story. "The kingdom of wisdom is joy in the Holy Ghost." Have they not held that man is a creature of sinful proclivities that make sickness and death, but if the temptations of sin are shut away from him he may possibly keep out of the hospitals and poorhouses and become a preacher or a Vanderbilt. But the ideal proclamation of the starry doctrine is "man came forth from the bosom of holiness. The kingdom of truth is not instruction in discriminations between good and evil, but simply joy in the Holy Ghost." Have we not held that if man does not employ his brother man and pay him wages to increase and manipulate material things, he will starve and freeze? The wormwood of the star that has fallen on earth today is the highest lamp of the testimony of Jesus that meat and drink do not come that way, but through joy in the Holy Ghost.

"Agree with the adversary quickly whilst thou art in the way with him." The only adversary we have is Jesus Christ. His doctrine is adverse to the church, the State, the school. His doctrine is the star that is wormwood to the current estimation of man concerning mankind.

Hospitals as Evidence

Do you suppose that hospitals are an evidence of man's acceptance of the doctrine of Jesus? No! They stand as monuments to our rejection of his doctrine. "I am persuaded by the Lord Jesus Christ that there is nothing unclean (or broken, or feeble or liable to accident), but to him that esteemeth the possibility of these things."

Having joy in the Holy Ghost taketh away the estimation, and man in his freedom and beauty is viewed as God sees him. When the second angel sounded, John saw a great mountain of fire removed into the sea. Between the sight of the New Jerusalem with its inhabitants as they are walking now, in our midst, stands the burning mountain of our estimation of men and things. The New Jerusalem is this earth and its inhabitants are these people. The second angel is the second lesson of the Christian doctrine on its last circuit. On its last circuit, you remember, this Christian science proclaims that the burning mountain of our own estimation of men and thing is cast into the sea by our willing letting go of our estimation of men and things. We have esteemed it of great importance that mankind be taught how to earn his living, keep temperate and behave honorably. We set that burning mountain aside into the sea of our acceptance of the doctrine that Jesus Christ in man is all there is of him, and he cannot be hungry, intemperate, or dishonorable.

Should Trust in the Savior

Do we suppose that it is evidence of our Christianity if we are distressed and anxious through sympathy for the unemployed, fearing they may be hungry and cold?

When the disciples saw the risen Jesus the found fish and bread and coals of fire prepared without hands. If I see the risen Jesus I shall see that the multitudes are to be fed and clothed independent of the factories and the farms. When the risen Jesus had fed the disciples he turned to the boldest one among them and asked: "Simon son of

Jonas, lovest thou me more than these?" And, the impetuous Peter, knowing that he meant more than his father, mother, brethren made answer: "Thou knowest that I love thee." Then again the question, "Lovest thou me more than these?" And Simon Peter knowing that he meant more than he loved praise and high estimation of man, made answer, "Thou knowest that I love thee." And deeper still the probe was pushed, "Lovest thou me more than these?" and with bold defiance of his own heart of charity and noble sympathy, understanding well that the risen Lord meant to ask him if he had got beyond thinking of men as hungry ignorant, and tempted, and could look upon them as they dwell in the New Jerusalem now, he cried out earnestly, "Thou knowest that I love thee." "Feed my sheep," said the risen Christ.

Never till joy in the Holy Ghost has superseded and ostracized all other thoughts even to the doctrine of helping the world can we feed the sheep. Are not 1,900 years if estimation of man from the outward point sufficient time for experimenting on looking at him as something unfilled with God? Let the third star be bitterness to who will. I, Peter, must let it be a lamp of joy unto my hitherto dark journey of life, that it is truth to say, that today there are none in want of fear only as I esteem them so. "Therefore I gladly cast the fiery mountain of my estimation into the sea of the doctrine of Jesus, viz., that all is joy upon the earth now.

The kingdom of God is in our midst. The Jesus Christ in man is all there is of man. This is truth.

Inter Ocean Newspaper September 17, 1893

LESSON XIII

REVIEW

Acts 26:19-32

Lessons that Lie Behind

There is a science of mind, a science of revelation, and a science of faith. There is a scientific way to handle everything. There are always twelve divisions in the circuit of each scientific manner of looking at things and principles. When one circuit closes another must begin. When the disciples of Jesus of Nazareth regarded him as a man among men, they saw him prepare their bread and meat; when they regarded him as an angel they did not see the preparation of their breakfast, but when they had landed on the shore, "they saw a fire of coals there and fish laid thereon, and bread." The circuit of observation of processes had closed, the circuit of beholding results had come. There is no doubt but that some cycle or circuit of time is now closing for the human race and another cycle is beginning. According to the science of revelation by symbolic language the reason of the close of the old circuit is because the answers to the prayers of the saints of the past are just now being fulfilled. The time of their fulfilling has seemed very long to the world, but under the dispensation of law each saint proclaimed the necessity for time, and the premise being times and seasons, there has been of course a science of times and seasons accompanying saintly prayers.

They did not tell of a moment, however, when all the tithes should be brought into the storehouse, and that time is now. According to the science of revelation by symbol, the angel that has had charge of the golden censer of prayers offered on the altar of life now beckons for the seven angels of the-new circuit to sound their trumpet calls to the world to look to Jesus Christ as a miracle worker among mankind again in a way adapted exactly to this age and mind.

The first six angels' calls are heard in the teachings of the lessons of the last quarter. The seventh is the sustained note of the lessons of the next quarter. This review lesson reviews the army of right doctrine both ways, forward and backward. Today we will scan the lessons that lie behind. Some of them express the call of the first angel, or the first statement of the new circuit of religion wherein man is taught that to be indeed risen with Christ is to find food and clothing and warm shelter miraculously provided.

As on the shore of Tiberias Jesus Christ looked as other men looked and the angelic food seemed as plainly fish and bread to those that ate it as what their wives and mothers had cooked for them, so on this circuit we are taught that our miraculous provisions shall seem as ordinary fare only, but nevertheless must be regarded by us as provided by the angels of heaven.

When the first: angel sounds his trumpet in your ears you will find yourself either reading some page that proclaims that it is the intention of Jehovah that all the inhabitants should share and share alike in the 'kingdom, or you will be found announcing it yourself. The result of this on the outer world will be great change in its financial situations, where a rich man's check is not cashed at a bank any more readily than a poor- man's check, and the rich men's millions slip through their fingers in spite of their precautions, while one new prosperity, and another and another, come into the lot of their hitherto unfortunate neighbors.

Joseph Cook's Fears

When the first angel sounded fire and hail fell from heaven. Fire and hail are great levelers. You can see for yourself that the great leveling time among nations has begun. Joseph Cook says that he fears that this leveling time as exhibited by our welcome to Buddhists and Confucians will stop our sending of money to the missionaries. It is very likely that there might have been some in the boat who thought that so many fish in the nets all at once would break the strands and they would have no breakfast at all.

Paul's experience with, the islander's who were in themselves stingy, as Mr. Cook fears some of our great churches may be, ought to be a lesson to every noble leader of the closing circuit of the doctrine concerning provisions. Not expecting anything from the islanders, expecting all things from heaven, Paul caused the Malta inhabitants to feed 300 of his companions .

His experience at Athens was a signal also that when the first angel sounds there is no high, no low; no scholar, no master; all is one. He showed that the divine wisdom, the providing principle, "is not far from every one of us". He showed that its action is both instantaneous movement and utter stillness. Nothing is so instantaneous as that which is in all places at the same instant, and nothing is so still as that which is everywhere, for it does not have to move on. The one principle being Good, and being in all places now, of course Hades, Satan, evil, are out of the question.

The Leveling Doctrine

The science of mind has for its first proposition: Mind is the ruling principle. The science of faith has for its first statement: I believe that Jesus Christ is now present. This is the first trump of the new circuit. It is the leveling doctrine.

The science of mind has for its second proposition: Mind is as great and free as it has courage to eliminate. The second angel sounded, and a great mountain, as it were, of fire was cast into the sea. The mountain of fire is the doctrine of necessity. Has not mind believed that it was necessary for men to be kept from evil? Has not mind believed that it was necessary for men to be taught religion in order to be saved from destruction; taught books and art to be saved from ignorance; taught physiology, hygiene, and surgery to be saved from sickness and deformity, taught trades and professions to be saved from poverty? This belief of mind in the necessity of life is the mountain of fire whose heat has made anxiety for the nations. The mind that has courage to eliminate this mountainous belief is great and free. Its statement of faith is the second lesson in miracle working, which reads: "I do not believe that Jesus Christ needs anything."

Paul brought himself into great freedom by confessing that he had believed himself to be under the necessity for bondage. This being a great belief of his, while the divine principle recognizes no bondage, he was free from that moment to preach what he liked. Some people believe that sleep is a necessity to them. Without sleep they burn with anxiety and dread. As Jesus Christ needs nothing; no man needs anything; for if Jesus Christ is here present, where is there that he is not present or needing anything?

The third statement of faith or the miracle-working mind is: I believe that the Jesus Christ in man is all there is of man.

The third proposition of pure mental science, is: Mind is as capable, wise, and strong as it has courage to say "I AM." This is the third sound of the angel on the opening of a new cycle. It is said by John to be the starry doctrine straight from heaven, but it is as wormwood to many men, he tells us, even in the churches, for they have believed that the Satan in man is as much of him as the Jesus Christ in him. Also, they have forbidden him to say "I Am" any higher than his appetites and passions have indicated.

This star, of course, is worm-wood to the teaching of business methods hospitals-building, and charity systems. When man hears the trumpet of this third angel he realizes that he is a transcendent being with all the powerfulness and wisdom he has courage to affirm. He, with the choice of what character, power, and doctrine he shall say, "I Am," hesitates to stop at being Socrates or Paul. He rallies the divine Jesus Christ within himself to affirm that the Jesus Christ in him is all there is of him. Paul so caught sight of the Jesus Christ in Agrippa and Festus that they acted nobly with him. The plebeian soldiers bound with chains to him treated him with love and preached his words in England and wherever else their generals drove them.

The fourth angel is the angel of prophecy. It sounded the message that the world must experience according to its faith. What is that good in man that rouses when you have faith in it? Is there a sick man whose health will not come at the call of faith? Is there a good life that will not obey if you love it? What is it that obeys? It is the best in man and nature. What is the best in you that moves at the orders of Jesus Christ? It is that which is himself. Do you wonder that the fourth proposition of mental science is: mind will body forth or demonstrate as much as it has boldness to command? It reminds of Napoleon Bonaparte's saying that the only reason the French Senate and army obey him better than others was because he was bolder in command. Do you wonder, if it is the best in you that obeys divine orders and the best in man and nature that obeys your orders that the fourth statement of miracle-working or faith has to be: I believe that Jesus Christ obeys me as I obey Jesus Christ.

Boldness in Command

Paul's miracles at Ephesus and his management of his jailor at Philippi, as well as his mighty command of the situation at Rome, show that he had boldness in command. The powerfulness of Jesus was that "he spoke with authority." And the measure of men's obedience to him measured their cure. The fifth, angel sounds and the beautiful doctrine of meekness is taught in its perfection of intention. How meek are you expected to be in order to be meek as Jesus Christ? Meek even to nothingness. This explanation of meekness, John says, is like scorpions to the people who cannot receive it. He calls it the sound of the fifth lesson. It teaches the belief of labor as no other teaching handles it, but it is, without doubt, the Jesus Christ principle. To the laborer it says, "Labor not for the meat that perisheth." Why not labor for our living?

Because on this circuit bread and meat and coals of fire are to be free gifts in reward for obedience, as the disciples, being obedient even to utter silence, had their food freely provided. As the widow, shutting the door in obedience to Elisha, found the cruse unfailing, even more than paying her indebtedness. Elisha told her to live on the money that was left after paying her debts by the direct supply of the angelic presence. He did not set her boys to work at a trade. He fed them from on high. This is the scorpion teaching to our world so welded to laboring for bread and fire, but with it goes all the indebtedness of man to man, or man to conditions.

Man is not only under the burden of obligations financial, but also under the burden of obligations tangible and intangible on other lines. He claims to be indebted to sleep for his rest, to friends for his happiness, to air for his breath, to water for his refreshment, to food for his strength. This is what the fifth angel's message or the fifth statement of faith, being received, does away with entirely.

Secret of Inheritance

It is really the revival of the mystic doctrine of bygone ages on "the All and the nothing." "The meek shall inherit the earth." The meek claim nothing, know nothing, think nothing. Thus they are under no burden of obligation, and this is the secret of inheriting the earth.

Pure water is invisible. Being liberated it would dissolve the very rocks. The center of the cyclone is Vacuum. The focus of the sun is still space.

"In such an hour as ye think not the son of man cometh."

It is the ability to withdraw utterly from all things and all people. "Woman, what have I to do with thee?"

The fifth proposition off pure mental science is: Mind is soul, spirit, mortal, immortal, heaven or hell at will, according to its decree. The fifth statement of pure faith, which is the miracle-working energy, is: I believe that the absence, invisibility and silence of Jesus Christ are his meekness.

Thus have the miracle workers of all ages been led on the fifth stair of their spiral ascent toward the Christ life to silence. Socrates spoke of two sciences which he was teaching, viz.: The science of oratory and the science of silence. "Stand aside in the battle of life, O warrior, and let the invisible warrior within thee fight for thee." The scorpion teaching that has goaded men on to what they ought and ought not to do ceases from stinging for all them that know that they are under no obligation to anybody or anything in reality. The angels talked with Paul when he felt this way even for one moment.

The Sixth angel sounds and all competition ceases from off the face of the earth". The angel of the four golden horns on the altar of life proclaims that heaven is entered through the doorway of a Name, and not by the strife of nations to reign and own the earth.

Power in a Name

Competition is said to be the life of commerce, but life, health, strength, support, defense are certain without strife when from the great river Euphrates, or human mind, the four angels bound therein for so long are loosed. The four bound characteristics of human life are approbativeness, amativeness, ambition, and acquisitiveness. Let free from human life the river becomes peace on earth, good will to men, and the armies must disband. Heaven is entered by a Name. "In my, name shall all the nations of the earth be blessed." Paul's holding to one name charged his clothing with spiritual power, so that crowds entered into health. That name "shall destroy the face of the covering cast over all people, and the veil that is spread over all nations." It is the open doorway, independent of law, into the heavenly city that lies here so close at our gates. The airs must part for sight, hearing, and touch to lay hold upon their rightful heritage.

1. *"Break open, ye airs closing thick to my sight;*

2. *Break, golden- red gates of the morning; There's*

3. *something, methinks, lying close to my hand,*

4. *That longs on my gaze to be dawning."*

The name that Jesus Christ himself used will toe the free gift to him who takes the fifth affirmation of faith: I believe in the name Jesus Christ as the open doorway to the kingdom of heaven. The sixth statement or proposition of mental science is: Mind experiences all that it names. That which mind names as cold it must feel. Sensation and mind are identical. If one does not know he is cold he does not feel it, and if he does not feel cold he does not know it. Whatever is named by anybody or whatever his mind accepts of the names of earth, he must realize. He is free to accept or reject. Therefore it is meet that the golden text of this review should be: "Faith cometh by hearing and hearing by the word of God." By much hearing of the name that is God, faith in that name rouses to white heat, melting the walls that hide the heavenly city we are now walking through.

Inter Ocean Newspaper September 24, 1893

Notes

Other Books by Emma Curtis Hopkins

- *Class Lessons of 1888 (WiseWoman Press)*
- *Bible Interpretations (WiseWoman Press)*
- *Esoteric Philosophy in Spiritual Science (WiseWoman Press)*
- *Genesis Series*
- *High Mysticism (WiseWoman Press)*
- *Self Treatments with Radiant I Am (WiseWoman Press)*
- *Gospel Series (WiseWoman Press)*
- *Judgment Series in Spiritual Science (WiseWoman Press)*
- *Drops of Gold (WiseWoman Press)*
- *Resume (WiseWoman Press)*
- *Scientific Christian Mental Practice (DeVorss)*

Books about Emma Curtis Hopkins and her teachings

- *Emma Curtis Hopkins, Forgotten Founder of New Thought* – Gail Harley
- *Unveiling Your Hidden Power: Emma Curtis Hopkins' Metaphysics for the 21st Century (also as a Workbook and as A Guide for Teachers)* – Ruth L. Miller
- *Power to Heal: Easy reading biography for all ages* –Ruth Miller

To find more of Emma's work, including some previously unpublished material, log on to:

www.emmacurtishopkins.com

WISEWOMAN PRESS

1521 NE Jantzen Ave #143
Vancouver, WA 98665
800.603.3005
www.wisewomanpress.com

Books Published by WiseWoman Press

By Emma Curtis Hopkins

- *Resume*
- *Gospel Series*
- *Class Lessons of 1888*
- *Self Treatments including Radiant I Am*
- *High Mysticism*
- *Esoteric Philosophy in Spiritual Science*
- *Drops of Gold Journal*
- *Judgment Series*
- *Bible Interpretations: Series I, II, III, IV, V, and VI*

By Ruth L. Miller

- *Unveiling Your Hidden Power: Emma Curtis Hopkins' Metaphysics for the 21st Century*
- *Coming into Freedom: Emily Cady's Lessons in Truth for the 21st Century*
- *150 Years of Healing: The Founders and Science of New Thought*
- *Power Beyond Magic: Ernest Holmes Biography*
- *Power to Heal: Emma Curtis Hopkins Biography*
- *The Power of Unity: Charles Fillmore Biography*
- *The Power of Mind: Phineas P. Quimby Biography*
- *Uncommon Prayer*
- *Spiritual Success*
- *Finding the Path*

Watch our website for release dates and order information! - www.wisewomanpress.com

List of Bible Interpretation Series with date from 1st to 14th Series.

This list is complete through the fourteenth Series. Emma produced at least thirty Series of Bible Interpretations.

She followed the Bible Passages provided by the International Committee of Clerics who produced the Bible Quotations for each year's use in churches all over the world.

Emma used these for her column of Bible Interpretations in both the Christian Science Magazine, at her Seminary and in the Chicago Inter-Ocean Newspaper.

First Series

July 5 - September 27, 1891

Lesson 1	The Word Made Flesh *John 1:1-18*	July 5th
Lesson 2	Christ's First Disciples John 1:29-42	July 12th
Lesson 3	All Is Divine Order *John 2:1-1*1 (Christ's first Miracle)	July 19th
Lesson 4	Jesus Christ and Nicodemus *John 3:1-17*	July 26th
Lesson 5	Christ at Samaria *John 4:5-26* (Christ at Jacob's Well)	August 2nd
Lesson 6	Self-condemnation *John 5:17-30* (Christ's Authority)	August 9th
Lesson 7	Feeding the Starving *John 6:1-14* (The Five Thousand Fed)	August 16th
Lesson 8	The Bread of Life *John 6:26-40* (Christ the Bread of Life)	August 23rd
Lesson 9	The Chief Thought *John 7:31-34* (Christ at the Feast)	August 30th
Lesson 10	Continue the Work *John 8:31-47*	September 6th
Lesson 11	Inheritance of Sin *John 9:1-11, 35-38* (Christ and the Blind Man)	September 13th
Lesson 12	The Real Kingdom *John 10:1-16* (Christ the Good Shepherd)	September 20th
Lesson 13	In Retrospection	September 27th Review

Second Series

October 4 - December 27, 1891

Lesson 1	Mary and Martha *John 11:21-44*	October 4th
Lesson 2	Glory of Christ *John 12:20-36*	October 11th
Lesson 3	Good in Sacrifice *John 13:1-17*	October 18th
Lesson 4	Power of the Mind *John 14:13; 15-27*	October 25th
Lesson 5	Vines and Branches *John 15:1-16*	November 1st
Lesson 6	Your Idea of God *John 16:1-15*	November 8th
Lesson 7	Magic of His Name *John 17:1-19*	November 15th
Lesson 8	Jesus and Judas *John 18:1-13*	November 22nd
Lesson 9	Scourge of Tongues *John 19:1-16*	November 29th
Lesson 10	Simplicity of Faith *John 19:17-30*	December 6th
Lesson 11	Christ is All in All *John 20: 1-18*	December 13th
Lesson 12	Risen With Christ *John 21:1-14*	December 20th
Lesson 13	The Spirit is Able Review of Year	December 27th

Third Series

January 3 - March 27, 1892

Lesson 1	A Golden Promise *Isaiah 11:1-10*	January 3rd
Lesson 2	The Twelve Gates *Isaiah 26:1-10*	January 10th
Lesson 3	Who Are Drunkards *Isaiah 28:1-13*	January 17th
Lesson 4	Awake Thou That Sleepest *Isaiah 37:1-21*	January 24th
Lesson 5	The Healing Light *Isaiah 53:1-21*	January 31st
Lesson 6	True Ideal of God *Isaiah 55:1-13*	February 7th
Lesson 7	Heaven Around Us *Jeremiah 31 14-37*	February 14th
Lesson 8	But One Substance *Jeremiah 36:19-31*	February 21st
Lesson 9	Justice of Jehovah *Jeremiah 37:11-21*	February 28th
Lesson 10	God and Man Are One *Jeremiah 39:1-10*	March 6th
Lesson 11	Spiritual Ideas *Ezekiel 4:9, 36:25-38*	March 13th
Lesson 12	All Flesh is Grass *Isaiah 40:1-10*	March 20th
Lesson 13	The Old and New Contrasted Review	March 27th

Fourth Series

April 3 - June 26, 1892

Lesson 1	Realm of Thought *Psalm 1:1-6*	April 3rd
Lesson 2	The Power of Faith *Psalm 2:1-12*	April 10th
Lesson 3	Let the Spirit Work *Psalm 19:1-14*	April 17th
Lesson 4	Christ is Dominion *Psalm 23:1-6*	April 24th
Lesson 5	External or Mystic *Psalm 51:1-13*	May 1st
Lesson 6	Value of Early Beliefs *Psalm 72: 1-9*	May 8th
Lesson 7	Truth Makes Free *Psalm 84:1-12*	May 15th
Lesson 8	False Ideas of God *Psalm 103:1-22*	May 22nd
Lesson 9	But Men Must Work *Daniel 1:8-21*	May 29th
Lesson 10	Artificial Helps *Daniel 2:36-49*	June 5th
Lesson 11	Dwelling in Perfect Life *Daniel 3:13-25*	June 12th
Lesson 12	Which Streak Shall Rule *Daniel 6:16-28*	June 19th
Lesson 13	See Things as They Are Review of 12 Lessons	June 26th

Fifth Series

July 3 - September 18, 1892

Lesson 1	The Measure of a Master *Acts 1:1-12*	July 3rd
Lesson 2	Chief Ideas Rule People *Acts 2:1-12*	July 10th
Lesson 3	New Ideas About Healing *Acts 2:37-47*	July 17th
Lesson 4	Heaven a State of Mind *Acts 3:1-16*	July 24th
Lesson 5	About Mesmeric Powers *Acts 4:1-18*	July 31st
Lesson 6	Points in the Mosaic Law *Acts 4:19-31*	August 7th
Lesson 7	Napoleon's Ambition *Acts 5:1-11*	August 14th
Lesson 8	A River Within the Heart *Acts 5:25-41*	August 21st
Lesson 9	The Answering of Prayer Acts 7: 54-60 - Acts 8: 1-4	August 28th
Lesson 10	Words Spoken by the Mind *Acts 8:5-35*	September 4th
Lesson 11	Just What It Teaches Us *Acts 8:26-40*	September 11th
Lesson 12	The Healing Principle Review	September 18th

Sixth Series

September 25 - December 18, 1892

Lesson 1	The Science of Christ *1 Corinthians 11:23-34*	September 25th
Lesson 2	On the Healing of Saul *Acts 9:1-31*	October 2nd
Lesson 3	The Power of the Mind Explained *Acts 9:32-43*	October 9th
Lesson 4	Faith in Good to Come *Acts 10:1-20*	October 16th
Lesson 5	Emerson's Great Task *Acts 10:30-48*	October 23rd
Lesson 6	The Teaching of Freedom *Acts 11:19-30*	October 30th
Lesson 7	Seek and Ye Shall Find *Acts 12:1-17*	November 6th
Lesson 8	The Ministry of the Holy Mother *Acts 13:1-13*	November 13th
Lesson 9	The Power of Lofty Ideas *Acts 13:26-43*	November 20th
Lesson 10	Sure Recipe for Old Age *Acts 13:44-52, 14:1-7*	November 27th
Lesson 11	The Healing Principle *Acts 14:8-22*	December 4th
Lesson 12	Washington's Vision *Acts 15:12-29*	December 11th
Lesson 13	Review of the Quarter	December 18th
Partial Lesson	Shepherds and the Star	December 25th

Seventh Series

January 1 - March 31, 1893

Lesson 1	All is as Allah Wills	January 1st
	Ezra 1	
	Khaled Knew that he was of The Genii	
	The Coming of Jesus	
Lesson 2	Zerubbabel's High Ideal	January 8th
	Ezra 2:8-13	
	Fulfillments of Prophecies	
	Followers of the Light	
	Doctrine of Spinoza	
Lesson 3	Divine Rays Of Power	January 15th
	Ezra 4	
	The Twelve Lessons of Science	
Lesson 4	Visions Of Zechariah	January 22nd
	Zechariah 3	
	Subconscious Belief in Evil	
	Jewish Ideas of Deity	
	Fruits of Mistakes	
Lesson 5	Aristotle's Metaphysician	January 27th
	Missing (See Review for summary)	
Lesson 6	The Building of the Temple	February 3rd
	Missing (See Review for summary)	
Lesson 7	Pericles and his Work in building the Temple	
	Nehemiah 13	February 12th
	Supreme Goodness	
	On and Upward	
Lesson 8	Ancient Religions	February 19th
	Nehemiah 1	
	The Chinese	
	The Holy Spirit	
Lesson 9	Understanding is Strength Part 1	February 26th
	Nehemiah 13	
Lesson 10	Understanding is Strength Part 2	March 3rd
	Nehemiah 13	
Lesson 11	Way of the Spirit	March 10th
	Esther	
Lesson 12	Speaking of Right Things	March 17th
	Proverbs 23:15-23	
Lesson 13	Review	March 24th

Eighth Series

April 2 - June 25, 1893

Lesson 1	The Resurrection	April 2nd
	Matthew 28:1-10	
	One Indestructible	
	Life In Eternal Abundance	
	The Resurrection	
	Shakes Nature Herself	
	Gospel to the Poor	
Lesson 2	Universal Energy	April 9th
	Book of Job, Part 1	
Lesson 3	Strength From Confidence	April 16th
	Book of Job, Part II	
Lesson 4	The New Doctrine Brought Out	April 23rd
	Book of Job, Part III	
Lesson 5	The Golden Text	April 30th
	Proverbs 1:20-23	
	Personification Of Wisdom	
	Wisdom Never Hurts	
	The "Two" Theory	
	All is Spirit	
Lesson 6	The Law of Understanding	May 7th
	Proverbs 3	
	Shadows of Ideas	
	The Sixth Proposition	
	What Wisdom Promises	
	Clutch On Material Things	
	The Tree of Life	
	Prolonging Illuminated Moments	
Lesson 7	Self-Esteem	May 14th
	Proverbs 12:1-15	
	Solomon on Self-Esteem	
	The Magnetism of Passing Events	
	Nothing Established by Wickedness	
	Strength of a Vitalized Mind	
	Concerning the "Perverse Heart"	

Lesson 8	Physical vs. Spiritual Power	May 21st
	Proverbs 23:29-35	
	Law of Life to Elevate the Good and Banish the Bad	
	Lesson Against Intemperance	
	Good Must Increase	
	To Know Goodness Is Life	
	The Angel of God's Presence	
Lesson 9	Lesson missing	May 28th
	(See Review for concept)	
Lesson 10	Recognizing Our Spiritual Nature	June 4th
	Proverbs 31:10-31	
	Was Called Emanuel	
	The covenant of Peace	
	The Ways of the Divine	
	Union With the Divine	
	Miracles Will Be Wrought	
Lesson 11	Intuition	June 11th
	Ezekiel 8:2-3	
	Ezekiel 9:3-6, 11	
	Interpretation of the Prophet	
	Ezekiel's Vision	
	Dreams and Their Cause	
	Israel and Judah	
	Intuition the Head	
	Our Limited Perspective	
Lesson 12	The Book of Malachi	June 18th
	Malachi	
	The Power of Faith	
	The Exercise of thankfulness	
	Her Faith Self-Sufficient	
	Burned with the Fires of Truth	
	What is Reality	
	One Open Road	
Lesson 13	Review of the Quarter	June 25th
	Proverbs 31:10-31	

Ninth Series

July 2 - September 27, 1893

Lesson 1	Secret of all Power	July 2nd
Acts 16: 6-15	The Ancient Chinese Doctrine of Taoism	
	Manifesting of God Powers	
	Paul, Timothy, and Silas	
	Is Fulfilling as Prophecy	
	The Inner Prompting.	
	Good Taoist Never Depressed	
Lesson 2	The Flame of Spiritual Verity	July 9th
Acts 16:18	Cause of Contention	
	Delusive Doctrines	
	Paul's History	
	Keynotes	
	Doctrine Not New	
Lesson 3	Healing Energy Gifts	July 16th
Acts 18:19-21	How Paul Healed	
	To Work Miracles	
	Paul Worked in Fear	
	Shakespeare's Idea of Loss	
	Endurance the Sign of Power	
Lesson 4	Be Still My Soul	July 23rd
Acts 17:16-24	Seeing Is Believing	
	Paul Stood Alone	
	Lessons for the Athenians	
	All Under His Power	
	Freedom of Spirit	
Lesson 5	(Missing) Acts 18:1-11	July 30th
Lesson 6	Missing No Lesson *	August 6th
Lesson 7	The Comforter is the Holy Ghost	August 13th
Acts 20	Requisite for an Orator	
	What is a Myth	
	Two Important Points	
	Truth of the Gospel	
	Kingdom of the Spirit	
	Do Not Believe in Weakness	

Lesson 8	Conscious of a Lofty Purpose	August 20th
Acts 21	As a Son of God	
	Wherein Paul failed	
	Must Give Up the Idea	
	Associated with Publicans	
	Rights of the Spirit	
Lesson 9	Measure of Understanding	August 27th
Acts 24:19-32	Lesser of Two Evils	
	A Conciliating Spirit	
	A Dream of Uplifting	
	The Highest Endeavor	
	Paul at Caesarea	
	Preparatory Symbols	
	Evidence of Christianity	
Lesson 10	The Angels of Paul	September 3rd
Acts 23:25-26	Paul's Source of Inspiration	
	Should Not Be Miserable	
	Better to Prevent than Cure	
	Mysteries of Providence	
Lesson 11	The Hope of Israel	September 10th
Acts 28:20-31	Immunity for Disciples	
	Hiding Inferiorities	
	Pure Principle	
Lesson 12	Joy in the Holy Ghost	September 17th
Romans 14	Temperance	
	The Ideal Doctrine	
	Tells a Different Story	
	Hospitals as Evidence	
	Should Trust in the Savior	
Lesson 13	Review	September 24th
Acts 26-19-32	The Leveling Doctrine	
	Boldness of Command	
	Secret of Inheritance	
	Power in a Name	

Tenth Series

October 1 – December 24, 1893

Lesson 1	*Romans 1:1-19* When the Truth is Known Faith in God The Faithful Man is Strong Glory of the Pure Motive	October 1st
Lesson 2	*Romans 3:19-26* Free Grace. On the Gloomy Side Daniel and Elisha Power from Obedience Fidelity to His Name He Is God	October 8th
Lesson 3	*Romans 5* The Healing Principle Knows No Defeat. In Glorified Realms He Will Come	October 15th
Lesson 4	*Romans 12:1* Would Become Free Man's Co-operation Be Not Overcome Sacrifice No Burden Knows the Future	October 22nd
Lesson 5	*I Corinthians 8:1-13* The Estate of Man Nothing In Self What Paul Believed Doctrine of Kurozumi	October 29th
Lesson 6	*I Corinthians 12:1-26* Science of The Christ Principle Dead from the Beginning St. Paul's Great Mission What The Spark Becomes Chris, All There Is of Man Divinity Manifest in Man Christ Principle Omnipotent	November 5th

Lesson 7	*II Corinthians 8:1-12* Which Shall It Be? The Spirit is Sufficient Working of the Holy Ghost	November 12th
Lesson 8	*Ephesians 4:20-32* A Source of Comfort What Causes Difference of Vision Nothing But Free Will	November 19th
Lesson 9	*Colossians 3:12-25* Divine in the Beginning Blessings of Contentment Free and Untrammeled Energy	November 26th
Lesson 10	*James 1* The Highest Doctrine A Mantle of Darkness The Counsel of God Blessed Beyond Speaking	December 3rd
Lesson 11	*I Peter 1* Message to the Elect Not of the World's Good	December 10th
Lesson 12	*Revelation 1:9* Self-Glorification The All-Powerful Name Message to the Seven Churches The Voice of the Spirit	December 17th
Lesson 13	Golden Text Responding Principle Lives Principle Not Hidebound They Were Not Free Minded	December 24th
Lesson 14	Review It is Never Too Late The Just Live by Faith An Eternal Offer Freedom of Christian Science	December 31st

Eleventh Series

January 1 – March 25, 1894

Lesson 1	*Genesis 1:26-31 & 2:1-3*	January 7th
	The First Adam	
	Man: The Image of Language Paul and Elymas	
Lesson 2	*Genesis 3:1-15*	January 14th
	Adam's Sin and God's Grace	
	The Fable of the Garden	
	Looked-for Sympathy	
	The True Doctrine	
Lesson 3	*Genesis 4:3-13*	January 21st
	Types of the Race	
	God in the Murderer	
	God Nature Unalterable	
Lesson 4	*Genesis 9:8-17*	January 28th
	God's Covenant With Noah	
	Value of Instantaneous Action	
	The Lesson of the Rainbow	
Lesson 5	I Corinthians 8:1-13	February 4th
	Genesis 12:1-9	
	Beginning of the Hebrew Nation	
	No Use For Other Themes	
	Influence of Noble Themes	
	Danger In Looking Back	
Lesson 6	*Genesis 17:1-9*	February 11th
	God's Covenant With Abram	
	As Little Children	
	God and Mammon	
	Being Honest With Self	
Lesson 7	*Genesis 18:22-23*	February 18th
	God's Judgment of Sodom	
	No Right Nor Wrong In Truth	
	Misery Shall Cease	
Lesson 8	*Genesis 22:1-13*	February 25th
	Trial of Abraham's Faith	
	Light Comes With Preaching	
	You Can Be Happy NOW	

Lesson 9	*Genesis 25:27-34* Selling the Birthright "Ye shall be Filled" The Delusion Destroyed	March 4th
Lesson 10	*Genesis 28:10-22* Jacob at Bethel Many Who Act Like Jacob How to Seek Inspiration Christ, the True Pulpit Orator The Priceless Knowledge of God	March 11th
Lesson 11	*Proverbs 20:1-7* Temperance Only One Lord What King Alcohol Does Stupefying Ideas	March 18th
Lesson 12	*Mark 16:1-8* Review and Easter Words of Spirit and Life Facing the Supreme Erasure of the Law Need No Other Friend	March 25th

Twelfth Series

April 1 – June 24, 1894

Lesson 1	*Genesis 24:30, 32:09-12*	April 8th
	Jacob's Prevailing Prayer	
	God Transcends Idea	
	All To Become Spiritual	
	Ideas Opposed to Each Other	April 1st
Lesson 2	*Genesis 37:1-11*	
	Discord in Jacob's Family	
	Setting Aside Limitations	
	On the Side of Truth	
Lesson 3	*Genesis 37:23-36*	April 15th
	Joseph Sold into Egypt	
	Influence on the Mind	
	Of Spiritual Origin	
Lesson 4	*Genesis 41:38-48*	April 22nd
	Object Lesson Presented in	
	the Book of Genesis	
Lesson 5	*Genesis 45:1-15*	April 29th
	"With Thee is Fullness of Joy"	
	India Favors Philosophic Thought	
	What These Figures Impart	
	The Errors of Governments	
Lesson 6	*Genesis 50:14-26*	May 6th
	Changes of Heart	
	The Number Fourteen	
	Divine Magicians	
Lesson 7	*Exodus 1:1-14*	May 13th
	Principle of Opposites	
	Power of Sentiment	
	Opposition Must Enlarge	
Lesson 8	*Exodus 2:1-10*	May 20th
	How New Fires Are Enkindled	
	Truth Is Restless	
	Man Started from God	
Lesson 9	*Exodus 3:10-20*	May 27th
	What Science Proves	
	What Today's Lesson Teaches	
	The Safety of Moses	

Lesson 10	*Exodus 12:1-14*	June 3rd
	The Exodus a Valuable Force	
	What the Unblemished Lamp Typifies	
	Sacrifice Always Costly	
Lesson 11	*Exodus 14:19-29*	June 10th
	Aristides and Luther Contrasted	
	The Error of the Egyptians	
	The Christian Life not Easy	
	The True Light Explained	
Lesson 12	*Proverbs 23:29-35*	June 17th
	Heaven and Christ will Help	
	The Woes of the Drunkard	
	The Fight Still Continues	
	The Society of Friends	
Lesson 13	*Proverbs 23:29-35*	June 24th
	Review	
	Where is Man's Dominion	
	Wrestling of Jacob	
	When the Man is Seen	

Thirteenth Series

July 1 – September 30, 1894

Lesson 1	The Birth of Jesus	July 1st
	Luke 2:1-16	
	No Room for Jesus	
	Man's Mystic Center	
	They glorify their Performances	
Lesson 2	Presentation in the Temple	July 8th
	Luke 2:25-38	
	A Light for Every Man	
	All Things Are Revealed	
	The Coming Power	
	Like the Noonday Sun	
Lesson 3	Visit of the Wise Men	July 15th
	Matthew 1:2-12	
	The Law Our Teacher	
	Take neither Scrip nor Purse	
	The Star in the East	
	The Influence of Truth	
Lesson 4	Flight Into Egypt	July 22nd
	Mathew 2:13-23	
	The Magic Word of Wage Earning	
	How Knowledge Affect the Times	
	The Awakening of the Common People	
Lesson 5	The Youth of Jesus	July 29th
	Luke2:40-52	
	Your Righteousness is as filthy Rags	
	Whatsoever Ye Search, that will Ye Find	
	The starting Point of All Men	
	Equal Division, the Lesson Taught by Jesus	
	The True Heart Never Falters	
Lesson 6	The "All is God" Doctrine	August 5th
	Luke 2:40-52	
	Three Designated Stages of Spiritual Science	
	Christ Alone Gives Freedom	
	The Great Leaders of Strikes	
Lesson 7	Missing	August 12th
Lesson 8	First Disciples of Jesus	August 19th
	John 1:36-49	
	The Meaning of Repentance	

	Erase the Instructed Mind	
	The Necessity of Rest	
	The Self-Center No Haltered Joseph	
Lesson 9	The First Miracle of Jesus	August 26th
	John 2:1-11	
	"I Myself am Heaven or Hell"	
	The Satan Jesus Recognized	
	The Rest of the People of God	
	John the Beholder of Jesus	
	The Wind of the Spirit	
Lesson 10	Jesus Cleansing the Temple	September 2nd
	John 2:13-25	
	The Secret of Fearlessness	
	Jerusalem the Symbol of Indestructible Principle	
	What is Required of the Teacher	
	The Whip of Soft Cords	
Lesson 11	Jesus and Nicodemus	September 9th
	John 3:1-16	
	Metaphysical Teaching of Jesus	
	Birth-Given Right of Equality	
	Work of the Heavenly Teacher	
Lesson 12	Jesus at Jacob's Well	September 16th
	John 4:9-26	
	The Question of the Ages	
	The Great Teacher and Healer	
	"Because I Live, Ye shall Live Also."	
	The Faith That is Needful	
Lesson 13	Daniel's Abstinence	September 23rd
	Daniel 1:8-20	
	Knowledge is Not All	
	Between the Oriental and Occidental Minds	
	The Four Servants of God	
	The Saving Power of Good	
	The Meeting-Ground of Spirit and Truth	
Lesson 14	Take With You Words	September 30th
	John 2:13-25	
Review	Healing Comes from Within	
	The Marthas and Marys of Christianity	
	The Summing up of The Golden Texts	

Fourteenth Series

October 7 – December 30, 1894

Lesson 1	Jesus At Nazareth	October 7th
Luke 4:16-30	Jesus Teaches Uprightness	
	The Pompous Claim of a Teacher	
	The Supreme One No Respecter of Persons	
	The Great Awakening	
	The Glory of God Will Come Back	
Lesson 2	The Draught of Fishes	October 14th
Luke 5:1-11	The Protestant Within Every Man	
	The Cry of Those Who Suffer	
	Where the Living Christ is Found	
Lesson 3	The Sabbath in Capernaum	October 21st
Mark 1:21-34	Why Martyrdom Has Been a Possibility	
	The Truth Inculcated in Today's Lesson	
	The Injustice of Vicarious Suffering	
	The Promise of Good Held in the Future	
Lesson 4	The Paralytic Healed	October 28th
Mark 2:1-12	System Of Religions and Philosophy	
	The Principle Of Equalization	
	The Little Rift In School Methods	
	What Self-Knowledge Will Bring	
	The Meaning Of The Story of Capernaum	
Lesson 5	Reading of Sacred Books	November 4th
Mark 2:23-38	The Interior Qualities	
Mark 2:1-4	The Indwelling God	
	Weakness Of The Flesh	
	The Unfound Spring	
Lesson 6	Spiritual Executiveness	November 11th
Mark 3:6-19	The Teaching Of The Soul	
	The Executive Powers Of The Mind	
	Vanity Of Discrimination	
	Truth Cannot Be Bought Off	
	And Christ Was Still	
	The Same Effects For Right And Wrong	
	The Unrecognized Splendor Of The Soul	

Lesson 7	Twelve Powers Of The Soul	November 18th
Luke 6:20-31	The Divine Ego in Every One	
	Spiritual Better than Material Wealth	
	The Fallacy Of Rebuke	
	Andrew, The Unchanging One	
Lesson 8	Things Not Understood Attributed to Satan	
Mark 3:22-35	True Meaning Of Hatha Yoga	November 25th
	The Superhuman Power Within Man	
	The Problem of Living and Prospering	
	Suffering Not Ordained for Good	
	The Lamb in the Midst shall Lead	
Lesson 9	Independence of Mind	December 2nd
Luke 7:24-35	He that Knoweth Himself Is Enlightened	
	The Universal Passion for Saving Souls	
	Strength From knowledge of Self	
	Effect Of Mentally Directed Blows	
Lesson 10	The Gift of Untaught wisdom	December 9th
Luke 8:4-15	The Secret Of Good Comradeship	
	The Knower That Stands in Everyone	
	Laying Down the Symbols	
	Intellect The Devil Which Misleads	
	Interpretation Of The Day's Lesson	
Lesson 11	The Divine Eye Within	December 16th
Matthew 5:5-16	Knowledge Which Prevails Over Civilization	
	The Message Heard By Matthew	
	The Note Which shatters Walls Of Flesh	
Lesson 12	Unto Us a Child Is Born	December 23rd
Luke 7:24-35	The Light That is Within	
	Significance Of The Vision of Isaiah	
	Signs of the Times	
	The New Born Story Of God	
	Immaculate Vision Impossible To None	
Lesson 13	Review	December 30th
Isaiah 9:2-7	That Which Will Be Found In The Kingdom	
	Situation Of Time And Religion Reviewed	
	Plea That Judgment May Be Righteous	
	The Souls Of All One And Changeless	

Made in the USA
Charleston, SC
15 August 2011